Spring St

Kenmare St

M Bowery

KU-744-143

WITHDRAWN

Police
Headquarters
Building

Old Police
Headquarters

Bowery
Bank Building

Centre St

Grand St

M Grand St

Lafayette St

Baxter St

LITTLE
ITALY

Hester St

Forsyth St

oward
St

nal St

M

Canal St
M

Shrine of San
Gennaro

Manhattan
Bridge
Entrance

Walker St

Museum of
Chinese in the
Americas

Eastern States
Buddhist
Temple CHINATOWN

Wooden
Pagoda

Confucius
Plaza

Bayard St

Columbus
Park

Pell St

Confucius
Statue

ver

Hogan Pl

Church of the
Transfiguration

Post
Office

E Broadway

Mosco St

Chatham
Square

Avenue
ngest)
ral
za

Thomas
Paine
Park

New York
County
Courthouse

Oliver St

First

Cath

liverpool
JMU

Learning and Information Services

Accession no		
	011620513 W	
Supplier		Invoice Date
	HJ	
Class no	391.009747 VIC	
Site	A	Fund code
		LSA4

NEW YORK FASHION

LIVERPOOL JMU LIBRARY

3 1111 01162 0513

LIVERPOOL JOHN MOORES UNIVERSITY
Aldham Robarts L.R.C.
TEL. 0151 231 3701/3634

Sponsored by

ECCO is proud to sponsor the V&A display, New York Fashion Now, which is a celebration of great design and innovative thinking. It provides a unique showcase for talented young designers to demonstrate to the world that you can push fashion boundaries, without compromising on quality craftsmanship. We hope that visitors to the display and readers of the accompanying book will feel inspired by this explosion of creativity, which gives us a real insight into fashion in 2007.

David Sleigh, Managing Director

First published by
V&A Publications, 2007

V&A Publications
Victoria and Albert Museum
South Kensington
London SW7 2RL

Distributed in North America
by Harry N. Abrams, Inc., New York

© The Board of Trustees of the
Victoria and Albert Museum

The moral right of the author
has been asserted.

Hardback edition
ISBN 978 1 85177 499 9
Library of Congress Control Number
2006936570

10 9 8 7 6 5 4 3 2 1
2011 2010 2009 2008 2007

A catalogue record for this book is available from the British Library. All rights reserved. No part of this publication may be reproduced, stored in a retrieval system, or transmitted in any form or by any means electronic, mechanical, photocopying, recording or otherwise, without written permission of the publishers.

Every effort has been made to seek permission to reproduce those images whose copyright does not reside with the V&A, and we are grateful to the individuals and institutions who have assisted in this task. Any omissions are entirely unintentional, and the details should be addressed to V&A Publications.

Designed by V&A Design
New photography for this publication has been created by Richard Davis, Paul Robins and Peter Kelleher of the V&A Photographic Studio

Endpapers reproduced with permission from New York City © 2006 Lonely Planet Publications.

Printed in Singapore

V&A Publications
Victoria and Albert Museum
South Kensington
London SW7 2RL
www.vam.ac.uk

NEW
YORK
FASHION

SONNET STANFILL

CONTENTS

007 **PREFACE**

008 **NEW YORK FASHION IN CONTEXT**

028 **SPORTSWEAR CHIC** INFORMAL ELEGANCE

ZAC POSEN
PROENZA SCHOULER
MARY PING
DEREK LAM
BEHNAZ SARAFPOUR

050 **ATELIER** EXPRESSIONS OF CRAFT

LOST ART BY JORDAN BETTEN
JEAN YU
MAGGIE NORRIS
COSTELLO TAGLIAPIETRA

070 **AVANT-GARDE** SUBVERSIVE STATEMENTS

SLOW AND STEADY WINS THE RACE
TESS GIBERSON
THREE AS FOUR
MIGUEL ADROVER

090 MENSWEAR
NEW VOICES, NEW VISIONS

JOHN VARVATOS
DUCKIE BROWN
ALEXANDRE PLOKHOV, CLOAK
THOM BROWNE

108 CELEBRITY
FASHION AND FAME

CHRISTIAN JOY
CRAIG ROBINSON
SEAN 'DIDDY' COMBS FOR SEAN JOHN

121 EPILOGUE

122 NOTES

126 SELECTED BIBLIOGRAPHY

127 ACKNOWLEDGEMENTS

128 INDEX

PREFACE

How does a designer go from being a relative unknown to becoming a tastemaker? This book explores the strategies of 20 New York based designers who launched their own labels in the half-decade between 1999 and 2004. Their start-up stories provide insight into how, in a notoriously fickle industry in one of the world's costliest cities, so many young hopefuls have come to prevail at this particular moment. A good number of these new arrivals began their companies around the time of the terrorist attacks of September 11, 2001. Designers, along with their staff, factories and retailers, struggled with the resultant economic downturn and the public perception of fashion as irrelevant and frivolous. Yet, as designer Behnaz Sarafpour, who established her label in the autumn of 2001, was to reflect some years later: 'I now think that it was the best time to start because the only way you could go was up.'[1] This statement, both provocative and counterintuitive, captures the keen persistence of the featured fashion figures.

Some New York designers take the route mapped out by the mainstream fashion industry, founding design labels specializing in commercially appealing womenswear. Others set themselves up in opposition to this model and create clothes that challenge conventions by virtue of their aesthetic, by the process of how their garments are made and sold, or by catering to a particular market niche. Key to the early success of some has been the focused support in recent years of the fashion press, retailers and manufacturers as well as the funded design competitions that help the winners pay their bills.

For many of New York's young designers, who are often financially unstable, this support has been essential. Without external financing, designers shoulder significant economic burdens along with the expectation to deliver creatively each season. In response to such pressures, some of the designers interviewed for this publication will have by now closed their doors and moved on. Still, the number of designer-led fashion businesses started and sustained in New York City at the turn of the twenty-first century is remarkable. *New York Fashion* attempts to capture this significant moment of design productivity, both within the city's mainstream fashion culture and outside it.

NEW YORK FASHION IN CONTEXT

East Village. 2005. Photo: Mara Catalan.

LIVERPOOL JOHN MOORES UNIVERSITY
Aldham Roberts L.R.C.
TEL. 0151 231 3701/3634

NEW YORK FASHION IN CONTEXT
AMERICA'S FASHION CAPITAL

New York overtook other fashionable American cities in the nineteenth century
to become the country's fashion capital. While cities such as Philadelphia, Boston
and, more recently, San Francisco and Los Angeles developed their own important
fashion traditions, by the late nineteenth century New York's busy port, large
immigrant community and varied retail establishments made it the country's prime
locus for importing, manufacturing, buying and wearing fashionable clothes. Spread
around two waterways, one of which, the Hudson River, provided access to cities
hundreds of miles inland, New York was ideally situated for commerce of all kinds.[1]
As the city grew and its residents prospered, their appetite for the latest styles
increased apace. By the early twentieth century New York's upper classes, and those
of other American cities of style, needed appropriate attire for the elaborate social
calendar of balls, dinners, weddings, private receptions and call-paying.[2] While
Parisian designs filled many a woman's wardrobe, New York-designed clothes
were increasingly in high demand.

   In the first three decades of the twentieth century, while many American
women still looked to Paris for fashion leadership, they also began to buy clothes
designed at home, with them in mind. As historian Caroline Rennolds Milbank has
written, American women's reputation for independence became emblematic of
their style as well.[3] By the early twentieth century, American women were attending
colleges and universities in greater numbers, entering the workforce and pursuing
active sport, and they needed simpler, less structured clothes that were appropriate
for wearing all day long. When, during the World Wars, American retailers had
to drastically reduce, even eliminate, their Parisian offerings, American designers
stepped in to provide the kinds of clothes that American women required. Design
pioneers such as Clare Potter (1892–1974), Vera Maxwell (1903–95) and Claire
McCardell (1905–58), along with others of significant talent, understood mass-
market fashion. Their successful combination of practicality and chic outfitted the
active, mid-century American woman, crystallizing American style at a key moment
in fashion history. Contemporaries such as Bonnie Cashin (1915–2000) and later
followers, including Anne Klein (1932–74) and Geoffrey Beene (1927–2004),
carried forward this democratic fashion tradition.

SUSTAINING A FASHION CAPITAL

BELOW LEFT A Bergdorf Goodman
holiday window, November 2005 to
January 2006, featuring an ensemble
designed by Maggie Norris. Corset:
tea-dyed, hand-embroidered textile,
Spring/Summer 2003; skirt: antique
powder blue silk with oiseaux hand
embroidery, Autumn/Winter 2000–1;
jacket: egg blue silk with antique gold
embroidery, Spring/Summer 2004.
Photo: Ricky Zehavi and John Cordes.

BELOW RIGHT Parsons.
Photo: Mara Catalan.

In the last quarter of the twentieth century a handful of fashion empires dominated New York fashion. Each of these designer-led corporations promoted a particular attire for their vision of the American woman; their omnipresence left little room for younger talents to flourish. But at the turn of the twenty-first century, roughly between 1999 and 2004, dozens of New York-based fashion designers struck out on their own. Their success has reinvigorated New York's fashion culture and points toward the city's continued vitality as a centre of American fashion production and consumption. Why have so many young fashion entrepreneurs prevailed at this particular moment? A host of factors is involved.

The ongoing patronage of the city's wealthy inhabitants along with the variety, luxury and cachet of its fashion stores remain important to New York's fashion industry. The upscale New York retailer Barneys is known for promoting emerging designers and directional design. The *New York Times* referred to Barneys' authority by describing the store as a 'metropolitan mecca of all that is fabulously new and covetable'.[4] Bergdorf Goodman is another New York retailer trading in high-end designer wares. Bergdorf's striking window displays, overseen in the 1990s and early 2000s by its influential window artist Linda Fargo, create magical, fantasy-world tableaux to entice passers-by (below left).[5] New York is also filled with the flagship stores of designers based elsewhere who seek to ensure a retail presence there.

Along with the reputation of its retailers, also significant is that New York is home to two of the country's top design schools: Parsons, whose Department of Fashion Design was founded 1906, and the Fashion Institute of Technology (FIT), founded in 1944. These schools are connected to the gritty reality of New York's fashion industry: they train, mentor and place many of New York's fledgling designers. The strength of New York's design schools is their position at the crossroads between commerce and creativity. These schools provide not only a grounding in the technical design process but also an awareness of how to design for a range of markets.

Combined with such long-established factors is a continued climate of general support for New York designers. This encouragement, even celebration, of local talent has been on-going since the 1930s when influential fashion figures such as Dorothy Shaver (1893–1959) – then Vice President of the retailer Lord and Taylor – and fashion publicist Eleanor Lambert (1903–2003) showcased New York designers through ground-breaking retail promotions and influential fashion shows. Following on from these early efforts, today New York's city government attempts to sustain a supportive environment for fashion entrepreneurs. With its red-carpet, celebrity associations, fashion remains a highly visible element of the city's creative industries. Generating an estimated $3.5 billion annually, the business of fashion in New York is also a significant economic force.[6] The sector provides over $150 million in annual tax revenue for the city.[7] Its twice-yearly fashion shows generate $100 million annually for New York City businesses.[8] Thus, City Hall needs to be seen actively proposing and backing programmes to sustain New York's fashion industry, which it does through a variety of educational, media and funding initiatives.[9]

Such assistance is particularly important to New York's shrinking number of garment factories. Manufacturing in New York still makes sense for some emerging designers with high-end products. Local production is highly skilled and allows designers to place the small minimum orders that foreign factories discourage. Local production also enables a designer to monitor quality easily and ensures

ABOVE Mary Ping, one of the 2005 Ecco Domani Fashion Foundation winners.

OPPOSITE CFDA/*Vogue* Fund finalists, 2004. Top row, from left: Libertine's Johnson Hartig and Cindy Green, Derek Lam, Cloak's Alexandre Plokhov, Peter Som, Dean Harris and Habitual's Michael and Nicole Colovos. Bottom row, from left: Behnaz Sarafpour, Doo-Ri's Doo-Ri Chung, Proenza Schouler's Lazaro Hernandez and Jack McCollough, Edmundo Castillo. Photo: Arthur Elgort/*Vogue* © 2001, 2004 Condé Nast Publications Inc.

a quicker turnaround time than manufacturing off-shore.[10] However, when a fashion business grows, its larger orders, too expensive now to produce at home, force the designer to manufacture abroad. This is one reason why, paradoxically, New York's fashion manufacturing sector continues to falter while its youngest crop of designers thrives in an atmosphere of renewed interest and support – a dynamic that has played out in other fashion cities such as London and Milan.

A further source of support for New York's emerging designers comes from the numerous and varied annual fashion awards. The designers who launched businesses around the millennium have benefited more than their predecessors from these awards, particularly those overseen by recently established award bodies such as that of the Italian winemaker Ecco Domani. Ecco Domani's Fashion Foundation (EDFF) is one of the newest award organizations, holding its first design competition in 2001. The Foundation not only links Ecco Domani's products with youth and creativity, but also credibly helps fledgling designers. The EDFF selects six designers annually from across the United States. The winners each receive a $25,000 grant towards producing a solo catwalk presentation during New York Fashion Week. Seven designers mentioned in this publication are EDFF winners, including Zac Posen, As Four and Mary Ping (left).[11]

Somewhat more established is Gen Art, a not-for-profit arts support organization that has showcased fashion talent since 1995. Its main annual fashion event, Fresh Faces in Fashion, ensures the winners' inclusion in a group runway show during New York Fashion Week.[12] In its first decade, Gen Art provided runway presentations for more than 400 new fashion designers.[13] Three designers in this publication are Gen Art award winners.[14] Judges for both the Gen Art and EDFF competitions have included influential industry insiders from the press and retail sectors, providing important professional contacts for award recipients.[15] Perhaps more significant than the prestige of winning, the publicity generated by both these awards and the fashion shows they fund helps bring attention to fledgling designers.

The most established of the fashion award bodies is the Council of Fashion Designers of America (CFDA). This not-for-profit trade organization, founded in 1962, has presented its annual fashion awards since the mid-1980s. Though without monetary value, the CFDA awards serve as career-boosting seals of peer approval, which are particularly important for emerging designers.[16] While the CFDA, Gen Art and EDFF awards have been important vehicles for young American designers, a decisively influential newcomer is the CFDA/*Vogue* Fashion Fund. Established jointly by American *Vogue*[17] and the CFDA in 2003, the Fund oversees awards that provide money and mentoring to one winner and to two runners-up. The Fund specifically targets emerging designers on the cusp of becoming smooth-running businesses.[18] The 2004 and 2005 winners each received $200,000, while the runners-up received $50,000; all benefited from assigned industry mentors. The CFDA/*Vogue* Fashion Fund judging panels have consisted of high-profile professionals from the fashion industry's press, retail and design sectors.[19] *Vogue* showcased each year's finalists in their 2004 and 2005 November issues. *Vogue*'s Editor-in-Chief Anna Wintour wrote enthusiastically about the 2004 competition:

This last year has seen a fantastic blossoming of New York fashion talent. It's been well over a decade since Marc Jacobs, Isaac Mizrahi and Michael Kors emerged and this is the first time

since that I have a real sense of a vital and
potentially durable generation of successors.[20]

Seven of the designers featured in this book, including Derek Lam, Thom Browne
and Jean Yu, have been Fund finalists.[21] Underwritten by Barneys, the apparel
marketing firm Kellwood and *Vogue*, the Fund has played a pivotal role in both
creating and sustaining that 'generation of successors' whose wearable designs fuel
New York's fashion industry. With 1.2 million subscribers, an estimated readership
of one in every twelve American women, and a powerful roster of top designer
and luxury-brand advertisers, on its own *Vogue* is a dominant force in New York's
fashion culture.[22] Crucially, *Vogue*'s links with the Fund associate the publication
with young, directional design, thus helping it remain attractive to advertisers and
also potentially creating advertising revenues by fostering young designer loyalty.
Because the bulk of most fashion magazines' revenues comes from advertisers
rather than subscriptions, efforts to attract advertising are usually a prime focus.
Further, by genuinely helping young talent, *Vogue*'s altruism secures the publication's
influence as a manufacturer of taste.[23]

    In addition to these awards, New York's twice-yearly fashion weeks help
young, emerging talent gain recognition. Designers – both those working in New
York and those based elsewhere who simply show there – value access to the
enormous American market that a New York catwalk show provides. Winning the
favour of the American press and buyers helps a designer navigate the complexity
of America's vast geography, varied climate and regional styles. Success at home can
be a launching pad to sell abroad, a goal for many of New York's young designers
who, though still emerging, possess global ambitions.

    A final contributing factor to the recent flourishing of New York's fashion
talent may be that Americans are tiring of high-street homogenization, with
sidewalks in New York's SoHo lined with many of the same shops found in
Minnesota malls. Such monotony may encourage upscale American shoppers to
take greater care dressing themselves. Their efforts to find the next new, compelling
product express a need, in the words of Barneys' Julie Gilhart, 'to connect to
something that is not everywhere'. One way to avoid the same-ness of a standardized
wardrobe is through the purchase of an emerging designer's innovative creation.

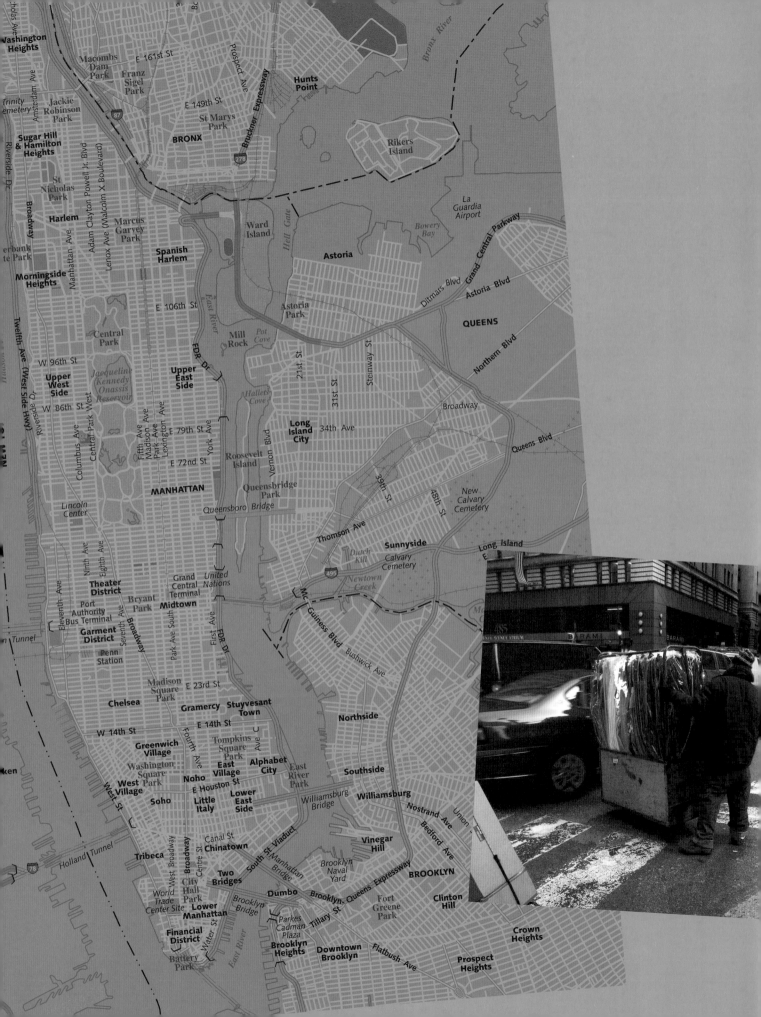

THE SHIFTING GEOGRAPHY
OF A FASHION CITY

LEFT Manhattan and Brooklyn map.
Reproduced with permission from
New York City © 2006 Lonely Planet
Publications.

BELOW New York's Garment District.
Photos: Mara Catalan.

Training, awards and press, and retail and government support have combined
with individual talent and drive to account for many of the recent start-up stories
of New York's fashion community. But how has this creative commercial activity
affected the city? Significantly, the designers' real-estate choices have contributed
to a shifting geography of America's fashion capital.

Emerging designers often set up their studios in lower-cost, 'edgier' locales,
far – in both distance and character – from New York's important retail centres
such as Fifth and Madison avenues and from the city's traditional garment centre
surrounding Seventh Avenue, bounded by Eighth and Fifth avenues and running
roughly from 42nd Street to 33rd Street (see p.014).[24] While 'Seventh Avenue'
was once a metaphor for New York's garment district and the American garment
industry as a whole, today's young designers now base themselves elsewhere.
From bustling Chinatown to arty Chelsea, from the *arriviste* Meatpacking District
to bohemian Brooklyn, these newly popular neighbourhoods represent the varied
alternatives to Seventh Avenue's former dominance. According to Derek Lam
(see *Sportswear Chic*):

Seventh Avenue is becoming less and less relevant. It's central and well-located but it's not attractive or stimulating.

Alexandre Plokhov of Cloak (see *Menswear*) agreed, saying, 'The traditional
Garment District is old-fashioned. It's a little bit depressing; it's too grey, too
crowded. There is no inspiration there.'

Downtown Manhattan offers a host of neighbourhoods attractive to the young
designer. Said Susan Posen, business manager (and mother) of Zac Posen (see
Sportswear Chic), 'When we first started we worked out of our SoHo living room.
If the buyers had been unwilling to come downtown we would have moved. But they
came.'[25] With 14th Street as the psychological demarcation line for Downtown, a
number of emerging fashion labels have located their studios below this symbolic
divide in areas such as Chinatown and the Lower East Side, and they continue
to open studios in long-established SoHo. Downtown designers perceive the lower
tip of Manhattan as a less commercial and thus perhaps a more authentic centre
of creativity.

New York's Chinatown.
Photo: Mara Catalan.

Three As Four in their studio
in Chinatown, 2005. Photos:
Mara Catalan.

A new frontier for young designers is **Chinatown**. A destination for large numbers
of Chinese immigrants since the mid-nineteenth century, from the late 1990s the
area hosted the workspaces of several young fashion labels. The design team Three
As Four (see *Avant-Garde*) were one of the neighbourhood's fashion trailblazers,
having lived and worked there since founding their label in 1998. Chinatown seems
impossibly far removed from fashion's power centre of retailers and press; its chaotic
street-level commerce creates the sensation of what Ange of Three As Four referred
to as 'being on our own planet'.[20] She praised Chinatown's relative lack of
gentrification by saying:

It's a little unspoiled. It isn't hip or trendy.
It keeps us real because we're with the real
people: the immigrant Spanish, Chinese
and Puerto Ricans.

She went on to describe their studio: 'It's in the heart of "stinky Chinatown".
It used to be a sweatshop. There was trash inside... it had no glass in the
windows, but we fell in love with its size, and with the light and the view of the
park out front.' With all its visible surfaces painted metallic silver and a high
ceiling punctuated with glittering disco balls, the one-room space reflects the
light streaming in from its large windows. The studio's artfully styled interior
contrasts with the bustling market atmosphere outside.

Further downtown is the **Lower East Side**, an area encompassing 2 square miles, with a complex history that earned designations as both a state and a national historic district in 2000.[27] From the mid-nineteenth century its tenements housed much of the city's Jewish and Southern Italian immigrants. Throughout the last quarter of the nineteenth century, these immigrants helped staff New York's growing garment industry. A century later the Lower East Side became host to a cluster of popular music clubs. Their arrival coincided with the reinvigoration of the city's music scene. These venues showcased the city's burgeoning blues, rock-and-roll and alternative music talent. Concurrent with the Lower East Side's music-led rejuvenation, several designers started their labels at studios in or next door to the Lower East Side. Bespoke tailor Craig Robinson (see *Celebrity*) was initially based there. Robinson dressed a number of the emerging New York-area bands that performed in the neighbourhood clubs. Although Robinson has since moved his studio to Lower Fifth Avenue (he enjoys his new neighbourhood's historic association with tailoring and haberdashery), he said:

The Lower East Side scene got us off the ground and paid the bills.

The neighbouring **Alphabet City** also hosts a small design community along with a number of music venues. Taking its name from the lettered avenues within New York's East Village, a decade ago Alphabet City was a crime-ridden, bleak 'no-go' area for many New Yorkers. Today its streets feature a handful of makers and smaller designer shops.

LEFT Advertisement for the East Village's Bowery Bar, now known as the 'B Bar'. Photo: Mara Catalan.

BELOW Meatpacking District. Photo: Mara Catalan.

Another recently transformed Manhattan neighbourhood popular with young designers is Gansevoort Market, colloquially known as the **Meatpacking District**. This area consists of parts of a dozen city blocks from West 14th Street on the north end down to Gansevoort Street at the south. By the turn of the twentieth century, an underground automated pipe system provided refrigeration to the meat- and poultry-packing businesses that became, after World War II, the area's main commercial activity. In the 1970s, nightclubs, particularly those catering to the gay community, began altering the district's profile. In the early 1980s the neighbourhood was further gentrified by one or two restaurants opening their doors – Florent on Gansevoort Street was a neighbourhood pioneer, opening in 1985. In the late 1990s fashion boutiques followed, such as the high-end, designer clothing emporium Jeffrey, which opened on West 14th Street in 1999. According to Derek Lam – a two-decade-long resident who located his design studio in the area in 2002 – 'When Jeffrey opened, people were sceptical. But [the boutique] made the neighbourhood a fashion destination. The other designers followed.'[28] So did the more mainstream restaurants and nightclubs.

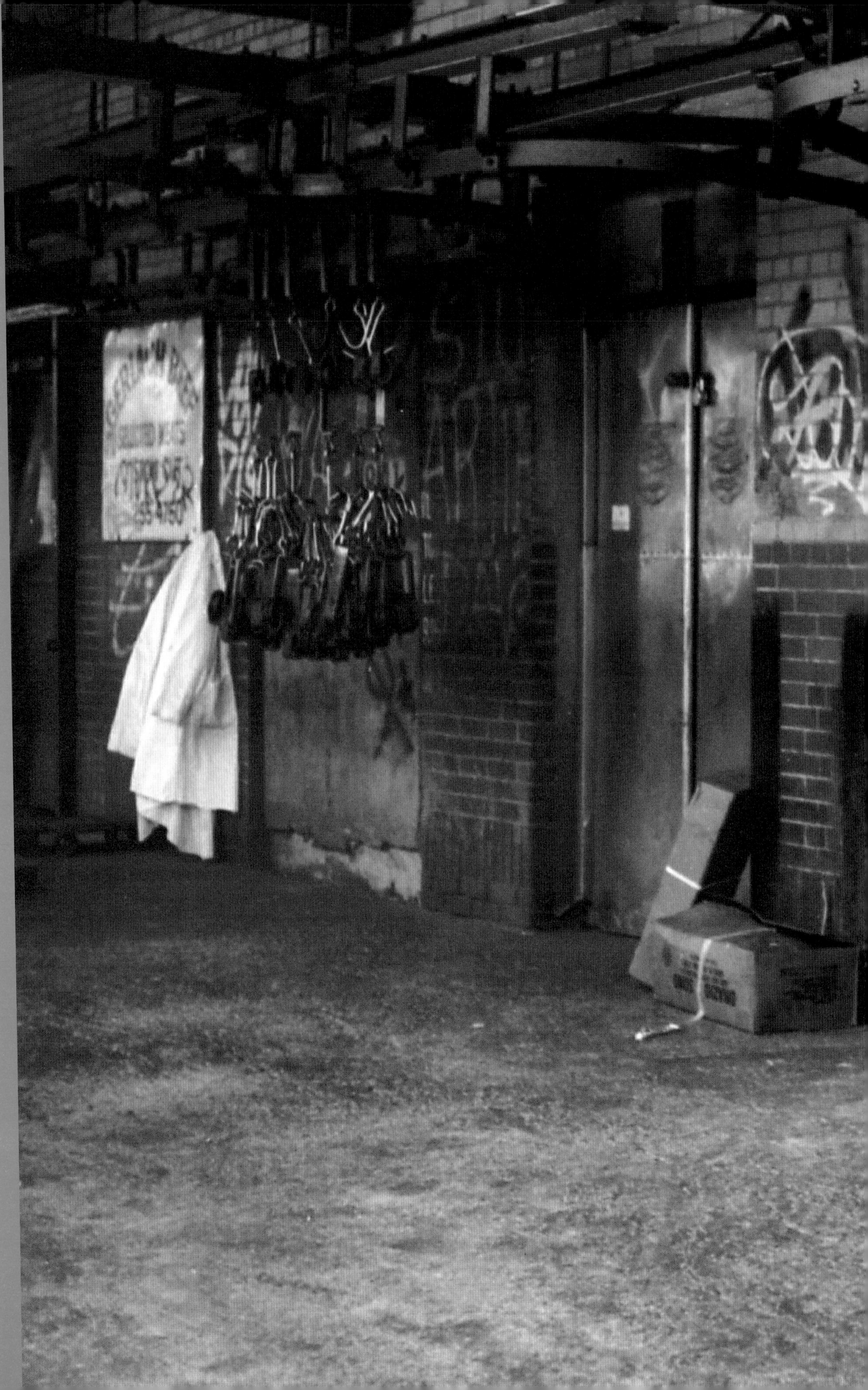

839
WALMIR MEAT
1 (212) 924 8164

Meatpacking District.
Photo: Mara Catalan.

The Meatpacking District's historical details, including cobblestone streets and the High Line (a 22-block-long disused rail bed), enliven the neighbourhood's industrial vistas.[29] Particularly characteristic are the metal awnings jutting out from the neighbourhood's brick façades, put there to provide shade and to act as anchors for the pulleys that load carcasses from trucks to warehouses. In 2001 there remained only around 25 meatpacking companies, down from the district's peak of 200.[30] Designer Daniel Silver of Duckie Brown (see *Menswear*) moved to the area in the early 1980s when it was still very much a functioning meat market. Silver said of the neighbourhood's once rough charm:

It was a meat market, so yes there were the meat guys, but at night there were also the gay transvestite hookers and the tough bars. It had a real neighbourhood feel about it.

In 2003 the Landmarks Preservation Commission declared the area a historic district, citing its buildings with 'special historical and aesthetic interest and value'.[31] Ironically, this very designation helped drive up real-estate prices, softening the urban edge and driving out the creative adventurers who helped make the area desirable. Derek Lam, who moved his operations from the area to Chelsea in 2005, said of this evolution, 'I do miss the grittiness.' In the view of Alexandre Plokhov

OPPOSITE Duckie Brown in their studio in the Meatpacking District, 2005. Photos: Mara Catalan.

ABOVE Jordan Betten in his studio in Chelsea, 2005. Photo: Mara Catalan.

(see *Menswear*), the area quickly changed from edgy fringe to theme park. Like Lam, Plokhov subsequently moved his studio to Chelsea. Plokhov said, 'When we first moved there it had a buzz and it was affordable. Now it's about fat money, fat people and the prices are stratospheric. We had outgrown our old space, needed a larger space but in [the Meatpacking District] the price would have been double.'[32]

Chelsea's street-level coffee shops, flea markets and upper-floor art galleries create a dynamic, appealing neighbourhood buzz. By basing their studios here, designers such as Lam and Plokhov can find spacious accommodation in its high-ceilinged buildings. According to architectural historian James Saunders, these structures originally housed light industrial activities as well as a range of what Saunders termed 'vehicle-related uses': taxicab garages, auto repair shops, trucking storage and warehouses.[33] Plokhov chose a former West Chelsea gallery on West 27th Street, not, he claimed, for practicality, or for the district's fine art associations, but because of the interior spaces of the local architecture. Plokhov spoke enthusiastically about his studio – its high ceiling, wood floors and spacious interior, which includes an office area, showroom and workshop, as well as a freight lift for deliveries. In 2006 Derek Lam moved his design studio and offices to Chelsea's 2.3 million square foot Starett-Lehigh Building. Lam was pleased to be based in an art district: 'We like to think that we're connected by a creative link.' Jordan Betten (see *Atelier*) has worked in a spacious West Chelsea loft since 1999. 'Chelsea happens to have a number of large lofts and warehouse spaces,' he remarked. 'The galleries moved in here for exactly the same reason.'[34]

Upscale **SoHo** is one of the more established locations for fashion studios outside the Garment District. In the 1990s designers began to follow the art galleries that had opened there in the 1980s. SoHo remains a popular address for designers wanting to be part of a vibrant commercial centre, and its art gallery community and high-end retailers provide a desirable backdrop. Zac Posen's studio borders the neighbourhood; the studios of established designers such as Marc Jacobs and Ralph Rucci are also located here. Jean Yu's atelier (see *Atelier*) is at SoHo's centre. Her shop and design studio occupy a tiny, jewel-like space at 37 Crosby Street. In contrast to chain-store encroachment onto the area's main arteries, Crosby Street shows that SoHo can still provide a measured, well-edited shopping experience.

Brooklyn's once undiscovered pockets are now popular and well trafficked. Designer Christian Joy (see *Celebrity*) referred to parts of Brooklyn as just as 'homogenized' – by which she meant that one finds there many of the same clothes and coffee chains – as Manhattan. However, sections of the borough still offer a quieter, community feeling than frenetic Manhattan. For many designers, Brooklyn's distance from suppliers, retailers and press would make the area impractical. For Brooklyn's bohemian makers, however, who tend to operate outside New York's fashion infrastructure, the distance is irrelevant. Christian Joy moved to her Greenpoint, Brooklyn studio in 2003 (above). In her view, Greenpoint has resisted the gentrification of neighbouring Williamsburg's independent designers, fashion boutiques and specialty shops. Joy's frank assessment does not skirt Greenpoint's rough edges:

Greenpoint is mainly Polish and Polish it has stayed. Its high point: a lot of good Polish food. Its low point: the alcoholics peeing their pants in the park.[35]

These varied studio locales chosen by New York's young fashion entrepreneurs correspond to a broad range of stylistic viewpoints. As the creations of the featured emerging fashion figures illustrate, New York's designer-led, higher-end fashion is a continuum that begins with appealing, commercial womenswear (the long-established foundation of New York's fashion industry) and ends with New York's relatively recent phenomenon of upscale clothes designed for or by a celebrity. Stops along the way include expressions of high craft, avant-garde aspirations and differing visions of modern menswear.

OPPOSITE Jean Yu in her studio in SoHo, 2005. Photo: Norman Jean Roy, originally published in *Vogue*, November 2005.

ABOVE Christian Joy in her studio in Greenpoint, Brooklyn, 2006. Photo: Mara Catalan.

ABOVE RIGHT Greenpoint, Brooklyn. Photo: Mara Catalan.

SPORTS WEAR CHIC

Behnaz Sarafpour, shirtwaist dress,
Spring/Summer 2005. Photo: courtesy
of Style.com.

SPORTSWEAR CHIC
INFORMAL ELEGANCE

New York fashion's latest generation of designers have established themselves quickly and by creating the kinds of women's clothing New York's fast-paced contemporary lifestyle calls for. Some of these newcomers have done so at a particularly rapid rate. Their forte: fashionable, dressy sportswear. While this American fashion industry term for informal ensembles of interchangeable separate pieces originally related to clothing for athletic pursuits, today this century-old mainstay of American fashion is worn to social events as well as to the office. Twenty-first-century sportswear, while it follows on from a tradition of appealing practicality, demonstrates an evolving sensibility. To a much greater degree than in the past, these clothes display the ornament, luxurious fabrics and eclectic design references desired by the upscale contemporary shopper. Such distinguishing details ensure that sportswear-inspired clothes continue to be the engine of New York's high fashion industry.

New York's fashion culture, like those of all the major fashion cities, is a complex of enterprises that only begins with designing and making clothes. While clothing is the focus, other relevant sectors include the media (advertising, celebrity clients and models, photographers, critics and fashion magazines), educational and professional organizations (degree programmes, awards and apprenticeships) and business (investors, retailers and customers). In New York, perhaps more than any fashion city, these sectors are interconnected to the point of being indistinguishable, which can help the young designers in favour and hinder those struggling for recognition.

In the years after the early 1990s recession, New York's young designers encountered a risk-averse lack of investment and support. In contrast, today's designers linked to sportswear's legacy, such as Zac Posen, Proenza Schouler, Mary Ping, Derek Lam and Behnaz Sarafpour, arrived on the scene at a time when both New York's fashion culture and its economy were ideally developed to welcome them. Two gained valuable connections by working for established designers before setting up independently.[1] With few exceptions, they all enjoy warm relations with both the fashion press and receptive retailers of international influence – soon after they established their labels key fashion stores took them on, including Barneys in New York, Colette in Paris and Harvey Nichols in London. All have received at least one influential, career-boosting fashion award.

The stylistic precursors to today's sportswear emerged – notably in New York – before World War II. For American designers at the time, the objective was, according to the late curator and fashion historian Richard Martin, 'problem-solving ingenuity and realistic lifestyle applications'.[2] **Claire McCardell**'s (1905–58) clothing illustrates the American sportswear tradition. McCardell excelled at creating simple, practical clothes that fit the indeterminate American dress code – neither formal nor informal – that emerged during the 1930s and then gained in popularity after the War. McCardell's contribution to this tradition was her ability to produce fashionable detailing in a mass-produced clothing line. McCardell's 1955 hostess dress (left) illustrates the stylish ingenuity to which Martin referred. Although intended for evening, the dress would have been worn in the less formal context of a drinks or dinner party at home. Thus the fabric is utilitarian wool and the dress's construction lacks the boning and petticoats of 1950s formal eveningwear. The classic sheath silhouette masterfully conceals the inclusion of side pockets, a functional detail typical of McCardell's sensible approach.[3] Several decades on,

ABOVE Claire McCardell, hostess dress, wool, 1955 (replica sash). V&A: T.77-1978. Given by Mrs Adrian McCardell.

ABOVE RIGHT Geoffrey Beene, jersey skirt, silk shirt, velvet jacket and knitted silk tie; 1974. V&A: T.30:1-4-2006. Given by Catharina Tinniswood.

BELOW LEFT Ralph Lauren, cotton blouse, cable-knit wool sweater and plaid wool skirt, 1981. V&A: T.509: 1-3-2000. Given by Jill Ritblat.

BELOW CENTRE Calvin Klein, cotton day dress, 1986-7. V&A: T.236:1&2-1997. Given by Calvin Klein.

BELOW RIGHT Donna Karen, black wool day dress and detail, ca 1985. V&A: T.98-1998. Given by the family of Baroness Birk of Regents Park.

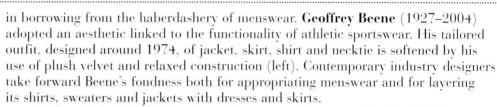

in borrowing from the haberdashery of menswear. **Geoffrey Beene** (1927–2004) adopted an aesthetic linked to the functionality of athletic sportswear. His tailored outfit, designed around 1974, of jacket, skirt, shirt and necktie is softened by his use of plush velvet and relaxed construction (left). Contemporary industry designers take forward Beene's fondness both for appropriating menswear and for layering its shirts, sweaters and jackets with dresses and skirts.

Full-scale individual histories of late twentieth-century New York fashion empires detail the contributions of **Ralph Lauren** (b. 1939), **Calvin Klein** (b. 1942), **Donna Karen** (b. 1948) and later **Tommy Hilfiger** (b. 1952). The precedent set by these sportswear greats, which today's emerging industry designers may or may not take forward, is that they each promoted a recognizable wardrobe for their vision of the American woman. Crucially, they based these wardrobes on stylish (even luxurious) but eminently wearable clothes (below). For these designers, wearable equalled comfortable, interchangeable and multifunctional. Through the sheer size of their companies, founded on clothing but broadened to include everything from lotions to luxury bedding, these sportswear-influenced designers dominated New York's fashion industry throughout the last quarter of the twentieth century. Early twenty-first-century emerging sportswear designers extend the customary combination of practicality and chic that Lauren, Klein, Karan and Hilfiger made fashionable.

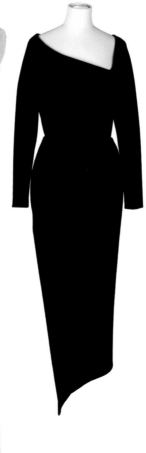

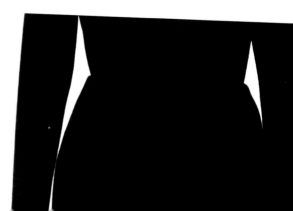

OPPOSITE Marc Jacobs, large-collared coat and quilted yellow skirt. Autumn/Winter 2005-6. Loaned by Marc Jacobs.

BELOW Narciso Rodriguez, orange knit dress worn by Karolina Kurkova, 2001. Photo: Raymond Meier, originally published in *Vogue*.

Forming a chronological and aesthetic bridge between these industry empires and today's emerging sportswear designers are **Narciso Rodriguez** (b. 1961), **Isaac Mizrahi** (b. 1961) and **Marc Jacobs** (b. 1963). Jacobs and Mizrahi were themselves 'emerging' in the 1980s, and Rodriguez started his label in 1997. Jacobs designed his first eponymous line in 1986. A day outfit from Jacobs' Autumn/Winter 2005–6 collection illustrates his career-long interest in layered informality with such ensembles as the elaborately collared corduroy coat, which envelopes a gold, high-collared shirt and quilted silk skirt (left). Similarly Isaac Mizrahi demonstrated skill in turning out simple, informal clothes from his very first collection, which he showed in 1988 (p.047). The early 1990s recession forced Mizrahi to close down his label, but in 2002 he entered into partnership with discount retailer Target to design a womenswear line. Target has annual sales of over \$45 billion and 1,300 stores across the United States,[4] making Mizrahi a powerful mass-market tastemaker. Narciso Rodriguez launched his signature women's clothing line in 1997 after a formative decade spent between Anne Klein and Calvin Klein. Initially based out of Milan, Rodriguez began showing in New York in 2001. He is known for simple, pared-down clothes, both for day and evening, with streamlined silhouettes (below). After seven years designing his own label Rodriguez had become sufficiently established to be asked to judge the 2004 CFDA/*Vogue* Fashion Fund competition.

ERPOOL JOHN MOORES UNIVERSITY
RNING & INFORMATION SERVICES

ZAC POSEN

At 21, Zac Posen was the youngest industry designer to start his own company, which he founded in the weeks before the September 11 2001 terrorist attacks. In spite of such timing, Posen entered quickly onto New York's fashion scene. Asked to describe the most important characteristics of his clothing, Posen named comfort and glamour, with 'comfort… first'. So although Posen's is a high-end, designer product with a strong focus on dresses for both day and evening, he acknowledges a debt to American sportswear's practical legacy, the element uniting Posen and the four designers that follow.

A native New Yorker, Posen attended fashion design courses at London's Central Saint Martins College of Art and Design. As a student he exhibited in 'Curvaceous', a Victoria and Albert Museum (V&A) display of Saint Martins student work inspired by nineteenth-century underwear in the Museum's archive. Posen's design was a full-length, long-sleeved gown composed of dozens of brown leather strips (left). The dress referenced traditional corsetry via intricate fastenings: hooks and eyes that are the only means by which one strip is attached to the next. Thus the wearer can adjust its shape as she wishes. Posen remarked at the time, 'My dress shows the progression of the changing silhouette from the bondage of Victorian life to women's emancipation from these confines.'[5] The dress came off display in time for the designer to include it in his catwalk show during New York Fashion Week in February 2002. Posen then donated it to the V&A's permanent collection.

Because of his British schooling and having had his work exhibited in a British national museum, a perception that Posen was English attended his entry into the American fashion industry. But in his ability to exploit both the industry's structure and his own good looks and charisma, Posen proved himself a consummate New Yorker. Posen understood that Americans are intrigued by Europe. He said, 'They thought that I was a European coming to visit New York for the holidays.'

Part of Posen's strategy was to step out deliberately onto the New York social circuit with Posen-clad models in tow. He used this tactic for some time before formally starting his label. In Posen's view the planned nature of such appearances allowed him to establish an image of independence while enjoying the media spotlight. He explained, 'I've been out there so much because I think it's important to communicate with your audience. Then you're not controlled by the magazines or controlled by the advertisers… If you're going to be controlled that way, you'll be banal.' The *New York Times* reported that Posen was soon a gossip column fixture, partying around town and around the world with celebrities such as Sophie Dahl, Naomi Campbell, Jade Jagger and Sean Combs.[6] Posen recalled:

We started with amazing hype from name and personality recognition. It drove this business and images of celebrities in the clothing drove it.

Soon after establishing his label Posen was the recipient of several key awards. First came the annual Gen Art Fresh Faces award in 2001. The following year Posen was one of six designers to receive the first annual Ecco Domani Fashion Foundation (EDFF) award. The $25,000 prize was helpful, but the press attention it generated was even more powerful.

While Posen's clothes continue to suggest the kind of flirtation exhibited in the leather strip dress of his student days, he has softened an early angularity by using volume, movement, supple fabrics, careful draping, and hemlines embellished with

ABOVE Zac Posen, hook and eye dress, Autumn/Winter 2002–3. V&A: T.213-2004.

OPPOSITE ABOVE Zac Posen and friends, 2004. Photo: Mario Testino, originally published in *Vogue*.

OPPOSITE BELOW Zac Posen, Empire State dress worn by Natalie Portman at Tribeca Film Festival, August 2002. Photo: © Rex Features.

embroidery or varied in length. Some of Posen's collections also include strong graphic prints. Posen's clothes are both appealing and flattering. Like most of his sportswear-influenced peers. Posen sells his designs across continents (North America, Asia and Europe),[7] the mainstream fashion press regularly features his work and his client list is celebrity-studded.

Posen views his post-September 11 timing as opportune, believing that, paradoxically, the period of economic upheaval that followed the attacks helped his fledgling company. It was his experience that financial uncertainty left many New York-area factories struggling and thus willing to work with young unknowns. This helped Posen to manufacture locally, a factor he considers critical to the success of his designs.[8] He said. 'I would never have been able to have done this without New York. There's no question that this is my city.'

LIVERPOOL JOHN MOORES UNIVERSITY
Aldham Robarts L.R.C.
TEL 0151 231 3701/3634

PROENZA SCHOULER

Like Zac Posen, Jack McCollough and Lazaro Hernandez started their sportswear-infused fashion label in their early 20s with little industry experience. They debuted their clothing line, called 'Proenza Schouler' to combine their mothers' maiden names, in 2002, both aged 23. Also like Posen, Proenza Schouler's rise to prominence was rapid. Barneys purchased their jointly made Parsons graduation collection and in under three years nearly 100 stores across the United States, Europe and Asia stocked their designs. In 2003 the Council of Fashion Designers of America (CFDA) presented them with Swarovski's Perry Ellis Award for Ready to Wear. That same year Ecco Domani selected them as one of the six winners of their Fashion Foundation award. In 2004 Proenza Schouler were one of ten finalists, and then the winners, of the CFDA/*Vogue* Fashion Fund award. Along with the $250,000 prize came professional guidance, formal mentoring and considerable press attention. These designers contend that even more influential than the money was the mentoring provided by Rose Marie Bravo, CEO of the luxury brand Burberry. Her advice addressed business strategies such as how the designers should work with their factories and price their garments. With such high-profile industry champions as Ms Bravo and *Vogue*, McCollough and Hernandez seem to have experienced only energetic encouragement from New York's fashion establishment. Consequently they perceive the city as helpful and supportive of emerging designers. McCollough remarked:

> One great thing about being a new designer here is that the editors and the stores are so supportive of young talent.[9]

Although most fashion designers work alone, McCollough and Hernandez describe their design process as a true collaboration. This teamwork may be one element that has helped such young talent succeed so quickly. Another is their choice of a clothing category on which to focus. For although Proenza Schouler do design elegant eveningwear, the designers are best known for consistently strong, polished offerings of interchangeable pieces with sportswear roots. Their 2003 collection included loose-fitting skirts, skin-baring camisole tops, shrunken waistcoats, trousers and pedal pushers or long shorts. One early ensemble comprised a grey silk skirt, a long, loose-fitting black T-shirt and an undersized brown suede jacket with scalloped edges (left). With colours and fabrics deliberately chosen not to 'match' so that the pieces were interchangeable, here is an example of the designers at their most informal.

   After their first few collections Proenza Schouler began working with more embellishment and higher-quality fabrics in keeping with their aim to build their label into a luxury brand.[10] Fashion journalist Suzy Menkes referred to the designers as 'America's new fashion generation', and described their Spring/Summer 2005 collection: 'The show was a feminine take on sportswear, given depth by intricate seaming and contrasts of surface textures, such as grainy linen beside shimmering Charmeuse.'[11] A jacket and skirt ensemble illustrates the designers' jaunty mix of fine fabrics (opposite centre): the sheen of the silk satin corset top contrasts with the tweedy finish of the prim skirt, and the jacket's bold floral print is an exuberant foil to an otherwise sombre palette. Proenza Schouler carried forward the themes of interchangeable pieces and informally mixed fabrics to their Autumn/Winter 2005–6 collection. Their catwalk presentation included a tailored, pin-striped wool jacket worn over a chain-mail tunic, a purple satin corset-top paired with grey flannel

Proenza Schouler, silk skirt and cropped suede jacket, Spring/Summer 2003. Photo: Monica Feudi.

BELOW LEFT Proenza Schouler, trousers, cropped jacket and shirt, Spring/Summer 2006. Photo: Monica Freudi.

BELOW CENTRE Proenza Schouler, floral printed jacket, silk bustier top and skirt, Spring/Summer 2005. Photo: Monica Freudi.

BELOW RIGHT McCollough and Hernandez with a model wearing one of their designs, 2004. Photo: Arthur Elgort/*Vogue* © 2001, 2004 Condé Nast Publications Inc.

trousers, even a nubby brown tweed cape worn with a grey jersey top and skirt of sparkling paillettes.

When McCollough and Hernandez first launched Proenza Schouler, they manufactured everything in New York-area factories. Although satisfied with the finished products they cautioned, 'The quality of your designs are good, as long as you're there.' However, after several seasons they began using more Italian fabrics. Such imports incur a hefty tax when brought into the United States for manufacture, making the logistics and costs of producing in New York prohibitive. Proenza Schouler then began to manufacture their knitwear, suiting, jersey garments and shoes in Italy. This list of product categories made abroad may grow in the future.

Few designers fit or remain within neat categories and it is possible that McCollough and Hernandez will leave their links to sportswear behind. Proenza Schouler's Spring/Summer 2006 collection showcased high-waisted dresses, matching trouser and coat ensembles and an increasing reliance on luxury materials such as guipure lace and hand-decorated linen (below left). Such dressed-up looks moved the designers further away from the practicality and informality of their early designs. When asked what direction they see themselves heading, McCollough replied, 'There are so many different roads a business can take. We're trying to focus on the season and the year just ahead. We're in our fourth shoe collection, we are thinking about a bag line, about menswear, about a bridge line and about freestanding stores. We will see where all this takes us.'

MARY PING

BELOW Mary Ping, gathered T-shirt, Spring/Summer 2004. Photo: Isabel Asha Penzlien.

OPPOSITE Mary Ping, Hound's-tooth sweater dress, Autumn/Winter 2005–6. Loaned by Mary Ping.

Like Proenza Schouler, Mary Ping (b. 1978) started her sportswear-inspired label at 23 with little formal fashion experience. Unlike the other emerging sportswear designers, Ping's design label is still very modest in scale: she sells her clothes through a handful of stores in New York, Los Angeles and Chicago, as well as several in Japan, and her label garners less press attention than those of her sportswear-influenced peers. Raised in the New York borough of Queens, Ping studied fine art at Vassar College in Poughkeepsie. After college Ping attended fashion design courses at the London College of Fashion and Saint Martins while interning with designer Robert Cary-Williams. Ping established her label in 2001. Working out of her Upper East Side studio apartment, Ping designs two collections a year. Ping designs both womenswear and menswear, but within the context of this chapter, the discussion focuses on her clothes for women.

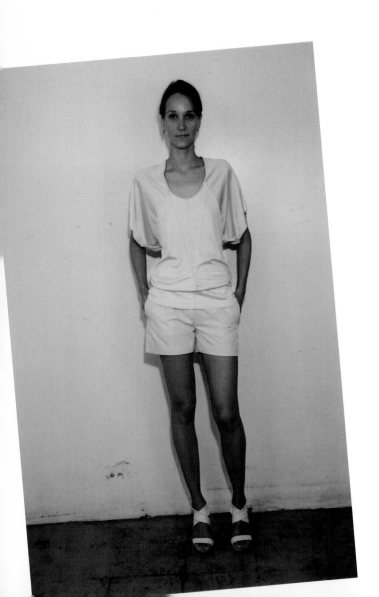

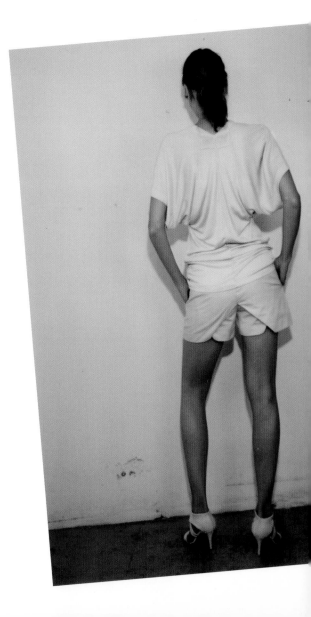

Ping's aim is to create a 'timeless, simplified wardrobe with a modern sensibility'.[12] Her designs are linked to the American sportswear tradition through their pared-down, versatile shapes and references to menswear-inspired basics, mix-and-match daywear and simple eveningwear. In particular, Ping has frequently experimented with the classic T-shirt. She has combined it with menswear elements such as a trompe-l'oeil waistcoat or a tailored jacket, designed it with an open slit down the back and elongated it for a minimal evening dress. Although such designs are spare, they are not dull. For example, a close look at other ensembles reveals the unusual design element that is often present in Ping's work. This could be the hem of a skirt that is knotted up on one side (Spring/Summer 2005) or a shirt slit and gaping at the shoulders exposing bare skin (Autumn/Winter 2005–6). What appears to be a basic T-shirt from the front is elaborately gathered and draped at the back (Spring/Summer 2004) (left).

Such construction details suggest that while Ping's clothes demonstrate a debt to sportswear, the designer's clothes are slightly more radical than her industry contemporaries. Ping's Autumn/Winter 2005–6 collection offered a reinterpretation of one of sportswear's cornerstones, the sweater. For her white dress with knitted hound's-tooth pattern Ping rendered the sweater exaggeratedly large (above). The garment extends beyond the midriff and stretches down to the knees, with sleeves so long that, if not bunched up, would dangle beyond the wrists. The size of the knit is also enlarged, so much so that the garment is see-through.

ABOVE Mary Ping, 'Bette' dress, Spring/Summer 2007, charcoal grey silk with circular side cutouts lined in double layered black satin faced-chiffon. Photo: Isabel Asha Penzlien.

RIGHT Mary Ping, stills from a film showing a model dressing for the day, Autumn/Winter 2002–3. Photos: courtesy of Mary Ping.

In addition to this subversion of design classics, Ping has experimented with unusual ways of presenting her collections. Although Ping shows her designs during New York Fashion Week, during her first four years she avoided the established, well-attended (and thus expensive for designers) Bryant Park tents. Instead, Ping sought out settings to match the 'feel' of each collection. She has chosen off-beat venues such as a masonic hall (2004), and the Lincoln Center in 2005, and has experimented with the traditional catwalk format. For Autumn/Winter 2002–3 Ping created a short film of a model waking up and trying on different Ping-designed outfits before going out for the day (left). Ping showed the film at the Daniel Silverstein gallery on West 20th Street in Chelsea. She projected it on a wall, and arranged for a musical accompaniment. Ping recalls, 'I wanted to save money. I also wanted to try a different format, something other than a runway show. I wanted to invite people into a cosy atmosphere to watch a film with music.'

In 2005, after four years in business, Mary Ping was one of the Ecco Domani Fashion Foundation award recipients. For a young designer like Ping, the award offered crucial press coverage and financial support for her fledgling business. It also attracted the attention of a handful of additional outlets interested in selling her designs. Although she welcomed these developments, Ping, who does not have a financial backer or business partner, said that the award brought with it pressure to be professional and presentable, and to 'get it right'. This meant taking care of the more mundane aspects of running a business such as organizing her computer files and tracking her designs more efficiently.

Unlike her industry peers, the small scale of Ping's business (she estimates her sales annual sales are under $50,000) means that she works almost entirely alone, with occasional sewing assistance from an aunt. In her first few years, she made most of the clothes herself, but now they are produced in a local factory. After attempting to outsource her pattern-making too, Ping determined she needed to retain control of making them herself. In navigating through these logistics and developments, Ping feels an affinity with her New York peers. She declared:

I love the New York designers and really admire their work. I think we all share the same desire to make quality clothes.

DEREK LAM

ABOVE Derek Lam, cotton jacket, cashmere tank and seersucker trousers along with examples of Lam's successful accessories line of bags and shoes, Spring/Summer 2007. Photo: courtesy of Derek Lam.

OPPOSITE ABOVE Derek Lam, embroidered crêpe-de-Chine skirt with 'laundered' leather jacket and cashmere scarf, Autumn/Winter 2005–6. Photo: Dan Lecca.

OPPOSITE BELOW Derek Lam, white cotton poplin 'tennis skirt' and shirt with grey cardigan, Spring/Summer 2006. Photo: Dan Lecca.

In contrast to Zac Posen, Proenza Schouler and Mary Ping, Derek Lam (b. 1966) was an industry professional with well over a decade spent at other companies before striking out on his own. Born in San Francisco to a garment industry family, Lam moved to New York to study fashion at Parsons. After 12 years working for others, mainly with established sportswear designer Michael Kors, Lam started his own label in 2002 at the age of 35. He presented his debut collection, Spring/ Summer 2004, during New York Fashion Week in September 2003. Once launched, Lam's designs achieved swift prominence. Influential New York retailers such as Barneys (which arranged to be the sole retailer to sell Lam's first season's designs) and then Bergdorf Goodman placed orders.

In 2004 Derek Lam was one of the winners of that year's Ecco Domani Fashion Foundation award. He said of the experience, 'In a short time they have made this award impactful: the award brings press, prestige and money. Also they follow up afterwards and ask how we're doing.'[13] That same year he was one of the ten finalists in the 2004 CFDA/*Vogue* Fashion Fund and was a finalist again in 2005. Lam cited the industry's retail and press sectors as crucial to his rapid recognition, specifying a coordinated, deliberate effort by the press and by stores to come together and support new designers. In the aftermath of September 11, Lam said, 'They feared that if they didn't, they might lose New York as a fashion capital.'

Although Lam's collections consistently include formal eveningwear and polished daywear, his clothes also demonstrate a debt to post-1950s American sportswear. Lam's focus is on designing outfits composed of separate, potentially interchangeable garments. The practical comfort of his elegant but informal daywear ensembles connects back to America's sportswear legacy. His Autumn/ Winter 2005–6 collection typified the mix of colours, fabrics and embellishment techniques that define the designer's casual approach to dressing up. For one outfit, Lam paired a red silk crêpe-de-Chine skirt featuring patchwork floral embroidery with a soft, 'laundered' leather jacket, whose metal disc buttons give the faint suggestion of uniform (opposite above).

A Spring/Summer 2006 ensemble of skirt, shirt and cardigan further illustrated Lam's skill in creating coordinated sportswear-inspired separates (opposite below). The skirt (which Lam calls a 'tennis skirt') and shirt were both made from white cotton poplin. Wrapped snugly with a cardigan, together they resembled that classic sportswear garment, the shirtdress. Historically, the early versions of this trim, flattering, essentially American style were based on a man's tailored shirt. The style coincided with the need for versatile garments intended for active sports, and its popularity was firmly established by the 1920s. By mid-century it became the quintessential expression of American informal daywear. This all-purpose garment remains, according to one dress historian, 'one of the most American of all fashions.'[14] By adding a V-neck cardigan (another contemporary garment inspired by early sporting dress), Lam offered a layered, flexible ensemble.

Lam acknowledged that his designs offer an unpretentious, nonchalant look but he also aims, as he put it, 'to capture a high level of technique and beauty'. Lam's materials tend towards the luxurious. For Autumn/Winter 2005 they included cashmere, chiffon, organza, satin, panné velvet and fur, and for the Spring/Summer 2006 collection, linen, suede and satin. In addition to supple fabrics, Lam's construction too is relaxed, although finely worked, with the designer favouring techniques such as embroidery, pin-tucking, lace inserts and pleating.

Having lived and worked in New York for nearly two decades, Lam feels a strong affinity with the city as a locus for design:

New York has always inspired my work. It's an incredible melting pot of different cultures, it is the crossroads of American, European, Asian and Far Eastern communities. It has always had a position where everything enters here, and ideas mix.

Although he takes inspiration from living and working in New York, for Lam, as for Proenza Schouler, manufacturing his clothes – with their luxury fabrics and surface detailing – was not viable locally. Lam attributes the American clothing manufacturer's struggle to a workforce trained in the classical tradition but with old-fashioned methods and outmoded approaches. Thus, when starting his business it was crucial, in Lam's view, that he use his connections with factories abroad. 'My first assignment was to take care of Italy,' he said, meaning that he needed to secure strong relationships with the factories best able to execute the details of construction and ornament in his clothes. Lam estimates that 85% of his collections are made in Italy, from the first prototype to the final garment. The factories he works with there are, he believes, technically advanced in terms of the production of luxury goods. Lam described their strength as 'continually developing old-world craftsmanship with technological advancements'.

Lam has succeeded since debuting his line in 2003. Sales went from $4 million in 2004 to nearly $10 million projected in 2006. His staff of 15 support Lam in his efforts, and now 120 stores (60 in the US, 35 in Europe, 25 in Asia) carry his clothes. In 2005 Lam opened a showroom in Milan to target the small European boutiques that sell upscale designer clothing. This strategy comes in response to the fact that over half of Lam's sales are outside of the United States. While he acknowledges that the New York stores that sell his clothes, such as Barneys and Bergdorf Goodman, are influential, he considers that his clothes sell best in the intimate atmosphere of the smaller, boutique-like shop. Said Lam:

It's about finding my own tribe, people that have an affinity for my work.

Lam also believes that selling his clothes in these stores makes good business sense for a fledgling company: 'When dealing with the large stores they need a lot of corporate special attention. We're a small infrastructure here.'

For Lam, the flipside of his initial success is his fear of becoming 'a novelty act' – a once-new designer who is then passed over in favour of the next fresh face. His industry experience, however, may contribute to the longevity of his enterprise. He declared, 'In the end we have to rely on *the work*. In the long term I draw strength from what it means to be in New York and how you can use clothes to express personality

Derek Lam, bustier dress worn by
Scarlett Johansson, 2004. Photo: Craig
McDean, originally published in *Vogue*.

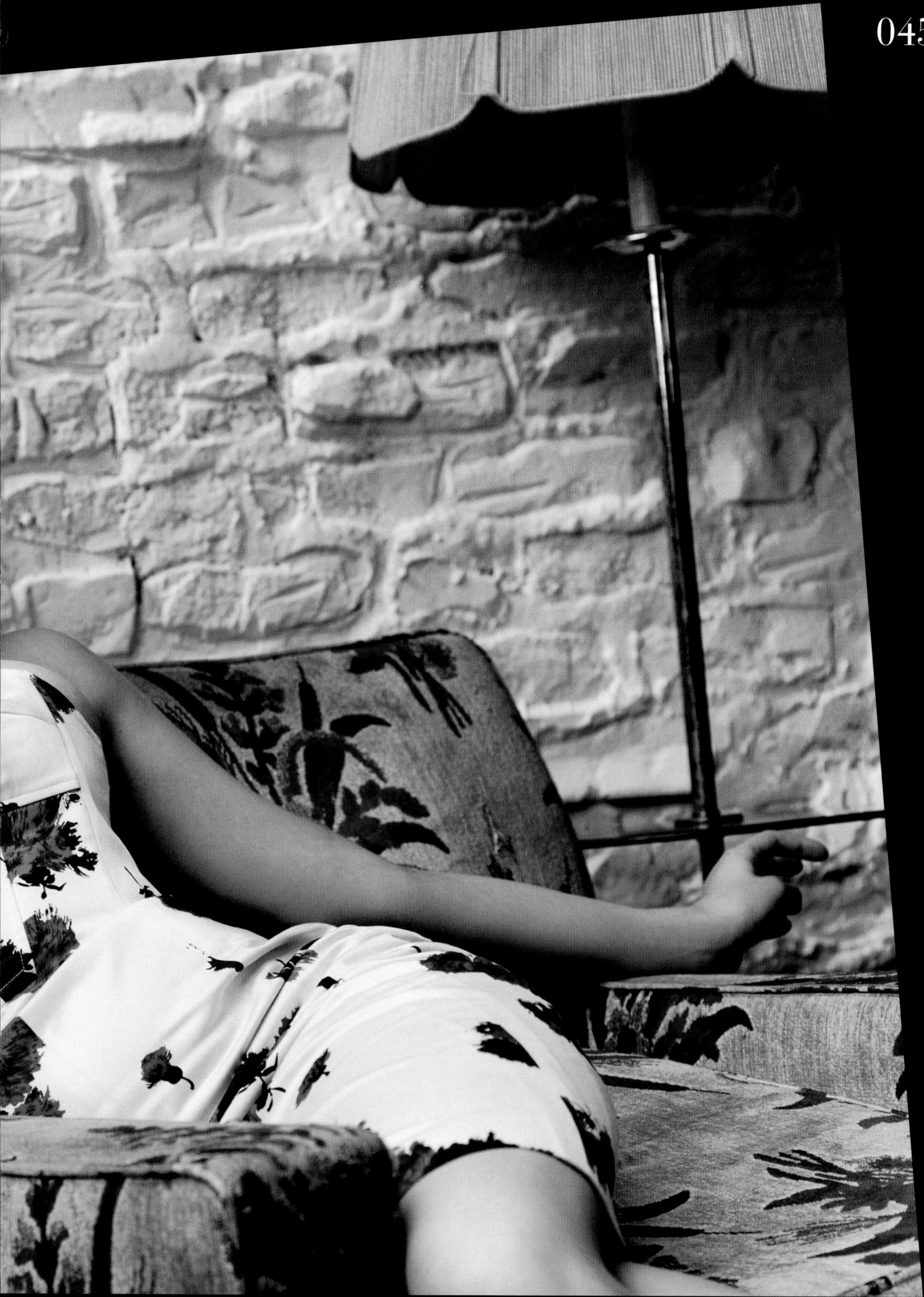

BEHNAZ SARAFPOUR

One of the few new female designers to establish a sportswear-inspired clothing line, Behnaz Sarafpour, like Derek Lam, spent years beforehand gaining industry experience. In this way she follows the path set by distinguished sportswear designers such as Donna Karan, who worked for 20 years for Anne Klein before starting her own company. Iranian-born Sarafpour grew up in the United States, attended high school in Philadelphia and graduated from Parsons in 1992. She worked for Anne Klein and Isaac Mizrahi and then designed the in-store womenswear line for the specialty retailer Barneys. She launched her eponymous company in the autumn of 2001 at the age of 30. Although Sarafpour does design eveningwear, much of it, like her daywear, can trace its lineage back to the versatility and practicality of mid-twentieth-century sportswear. What is significant about Sarafpour is her reinterpretation of classic sportswear looks as well as an ability to infuse eveningwear with a nonchalant sportswear spirit. In Sarafpour's view, her aesthetic 'has a basic sportswear mentality behind it, which is very much about interchangeable, functional clothing.'[15]

After years spent designing for someone else, Sarafpour wanted to make clothes according to her own creative vision. Describing the motivation to start her own company, she said:

I really wanted a personal, creative outlet for myself, and I didn't really care so much if anybody would come to buy it; I just wanted a place that wasn't about being commercial, a little place in my life where I could do what I felt creatively excited about without any pressure of merchandising and selling and all that. But the funny thing is, it actually succeeded.

The launch of Sarafpour's own label coincided roughly with the terrorist attacks of September 11. She recollected the early months, a period when she worked with one assistant out of her apartment: 'When I started out on my own the economy was very bad. A lot of designers were going out of business or just not doing as well as they had been. But I now think that it was the best time to start a new company because the only way you could go was up.' Sarafpour decided initially to remain deliberately small and exclusive. During her first year in business she sold the collection to one only store, Barneys. Then, 'the minute we opened up our distribution it doubled, and the year after that it doubled, and so it started taking off very fast.' The designer received early fashion editorial support from *Vogue*: she was a 2004 CFDA/*Vogue* Fashion Fund finalist. By 2006, with help from a staff of a half dozen, she was selling her clothes in roughly 50 stores in the United States, Europe and Asia with annual sales of roughly $2 million per year.[16]

Although Sarafpour studied in New York, worked for its fashion establishment and now makes the kinds of clothes that sustain its fashion industry, she views being a New York designer with some ambivalence. Unlike Zac Posen, who produces many things locally, Sarafpour, manufactures most of her designs abroad, as does Derek Lam, and increasingly Proenza Schouler. She explains why: 'I always feel that people who work in Paris or Milan really have such an edge over us in terms of

Isaac Mizrahi, shown with Sarah Jessica
Parker wearing a Behnaz Sarafpour lace
dress, Spring/Summer 2002. Photo: Mario
Testino, originally published in *Vogue*.

what they have available to them – very closely.' She went on to describe what she views as a lack of viable New York-area resources:

I feel that we would be better if we had the sort of craftsmen and factories that are in Europe. One or two generations ago, I think that American fashion was very separate from European fashion. Now with the Internet and more and more publicity we find ourselves in the position where we can compete much more directly on the same level with the Europeans but, at the same time, not really having the resources that the Europeans have at their fingertips.

While grateful for America's enormous appetite for designer fashion, Sarafpour lamented the challenges of designing clothes that are best produced overseas. She said, 'What is difficult about working with suppliers based in Europe is that everything that goes into production comes from that kind of physical distance.' Manufacturing clothing abroad can be complicated; it means a designer must travel a great deal and also be in constant communication with the companies that supply their fabrics and trimmings.

ABOVE Behnaz Sarafpour, CFDA/*Vogue* Fashion Fund presentation, 2004. Photo: Arthur Elgort/*Vogue* © 2001, 2004 Condé Nast Publications Inc.

OPPOSITE LEFT Behnaz Sarafpour, pleated silk skirt and cardigan, Autumn/Winter 2004–5. Photo: courtesy of Style.com.

OPPOSITE RIGHT Behnaz Sarafpour, evening dress with tulle skirt, Autumn/Winter 2004–5. Photo: courtesy of Behnaz Sarafpour.

While her clothes may be manufactured abroad, Sarafpour's design aesthetic is linked to the versatility and practicality of mid-twentieth-century American sportswear. Even when dressy, her clothes are functional and easy to move in. Her 'shirtwaist' dress from Spring/Summer 2005 (see p.029), like Derek Lam's (see p.043), is as straightforward a garment as McCardell's 1955 hostess dress (see p.030). Sarafpour kept the classic shirtdress' crisp cotton fabric and sharply tailored collar but modernized the original with a few deft changes: customarily buttoned down the centre front, it now has a wrap-around design. And instead of the usual pockets, the designer has merely suggested them with trompe-l'oeil pocket flaps. By belting the dress with an eclectic, obi-like, silk sash, Sarafpour updated a sportswear staple.

Although Sarafpour borrows from menswear, her designs are resolutely feminine. Her Autumn/Winter 2004–5 collection included a variety of refined and (in true sportswear spirit) interchangeable options: lace-edged camisoles, satin-trimmed sweaters and delicate, printed silk tops. She used the sportswear technique of layering these pieces with jackets, wraps and shawls and combining them with trousers or skirts. Her outfit of a grey silk skirt with white cotton shirt and pale yellow cardigan nicely illustrates the interchangability of her sportswear-inspired designs (opposite left). Since the variety of materials (wool, cotton and silk) and complementary colours were designed not to 'match', the individual pieces could easily be worn with other things. Additionally, the soft silk of the knife-pleated skirt, although shown as daywear, could also be worn as eveningwear. She described the woman who wears her clothes as 'someone who has an appreciation for luxury and who wants something that's going to be different'.

Although Sarafpour uses words such as 'luxury' in reference to her designs, she described even her most delicate styles as 'sporty' in their informality. An evening dress from Autumn/Winter 2003–4 is one example (opposite right). For this, Sarafpour attached a full skirt of fine white tulle to a drop-waisted bodice of plain linen. Sarafpour, who enjoys looking at historical fashion in museum archives, reveals the inspiration for the dress: 'For this design I used a 1950s Christian Dior corset and slip that was made to go under an evening gown. It should really be an under-dress but I wanted to show the incredible work that was underneath what you were supposed to see. Those undergarments just became the outer clothes.' Sarafpour transformed the hard carapace of Dior's boned bodices into a soft, weightless version of the original design. Although the designer referenced mid-century eveningwear for inspiration, unlike those formal constructions her bodice is not boned, its edges are unfinished and the seams exaggerated. As a final, slightly subversive touch, Sarafpour placed the weight-supporting ribbon, which couturiers once employed in a dress's interior, visibly on the outside. The result is the essence of American sportswear – dressed-up clothes with an informal spirit. An observation Sarafpour made about this garment could easily apply to the work of all the designers working within the industry's favourite clothing category: 'To me, that's very sporty, very American because it is done in an easy way.'

With their early success, Zac Posen, Proenza Schouler, Mary Ping, Derek Lam and Behnaz Sarafpour, along with their sportswear-chic clothes, are emblematic of New York's fast-paced rhythm. In the words of Zac Posen, 'New York is a dramatic city. It's high drama, it's high energy. I don't think there is a place that runs faster. I think it's important to have the costumes to dress for that.'

ATELIER

Jean Yu, chiffon dress. Spring/Summer
2006. Photo: Kenny Jossick.

ATELIER
EXPRESSIONS OF CRAFT

BELOW Charles James, black worsted wool coat with white cotton piqué collar, c.1938. V&A: T.291-1978. Given by Miss Philippa Barnes.

OPPOSITE Ralph Rucci, cashmere suit with leather detailing, Autumn/Winter 2005–6. Loan: Ralph Rucci.

Complementing the broad appeal of New York's emerging designer sportswear are the garments of designers deeply committed to a more specialized interest: the traditional techniques of making clothes. Their highly skilled craftsmanship and personal attention to clients embody an atelier approach, reflecting the sense of an artisan's workshop rather than an enterprise geared to commercial production. New York's ateliers are typically small businesses. Crucially these designers are preoccupied with using special materials and techniques to create made-to-measure garments for clients who appreciate such design distinction. The atelier approach avoids fashion fads and limits distribution to a select group of outlets, thus creating clothes that few people will own. And these are the designers who tend – with some exceptions – to operate outside the fashion system by showing their designs or seasonal collections in their studios rather than on the catwalk.

Sportswear's dominance can overshadow other elements of New York's fashion culture, and while the mid-twentieth-century boom in mass-produced separates continues to drive American fashion, there is a New York precedent for atelier designers – represented here by Jordan Betten, Jean Yu, Maggie Norris and Costello Tagliapietra – and their zealous involvement with the details of crafting clothes. An early example is the English-born, Manhattan-based **Charles James** (1906–78). Perhaps best known for his extravagant evening gowns, James also demonstrated absolute mastery of cut and construction in the simplicity of his garments, such as in a black wool coat around 1938 (left). Its double-layered, standing collar is achieved by ingenious folds across the bodice. A half-century later, **Ralph Rucci** (b. 1957) focuses on craftsmanship and technique. Rucci has been presenting collections since 1981 and designing a couture line since 2002. His cashmere suit with leather embroidery (Autumn/Winter 2005–6) exemplifies the designer's considered choice of materials and the precision of his studio's hand-worked embroidery (opposite). Like Rucci, for over two decades **Isobel Toledo** (b. 1961) has made clothes distinguished by a focus on the particulars of cut and form. A vivid example is her 'hermaphrodite' dress of Spring/Summer 1998. A series of rings stitched around the garment ensure that, when worn, the dress falls about the body in soft, pouch-like folds (see p.054). The clothes of **Yeohlee Teng** have also set standards for a designer's treatment of form and materials. Yeohlee's designs, though rooted in the ease of sportswear, combine luxurious materials with economical construction (see p.055).

RIGHT Isobel Toledo, Hermaphrodite dress, 1998. Photo: Dan Lecca.

OPPOSITE RIGHT Yeohlee Teng, silk skirt with top, Autumn/Winter 1999–2000. V&A: T. 82:1&2-2001. Given by Yeohlee Teng.

LOST ART BY JORDAN BETTEN

Jordan Betten, who with his small team of artisans works using mainly leather, suede and other animal skins, is the most specialized of the recently established atelier designers. Designing under the Lost Art label, Betten (b. 1970) and his team create bespoke garments employing traditional leather-making techniques such as lacing, fringing and beading. Betten spent much of his rural Connecticut childhood outdoors with his hunter-trapper father, an experience informing his interest in designing with pelts and skins. Although Betten works with the products of nature, he values the cosmopolitan thrum of Manhattan life. He uses his West Chelsea workshop both for designing and attending to clients. He revels in the real-life theatre of the streets outside. Betten said:

I love New York because as an artist I draw inspiration from my surroundings. Every day in New York, when you hit the streets you see something you would never expect to see.[1]

After college and several years of modelling, Betten founded Lost Art in 1997 when he was 27. With encouragement and patronage from the established designer Anna Sui, he taught himself the techniques of working with leather, first by making leather bags and then experimenting with clothing. Betten also received early encouragement from Gen Art, the not-for-profit arts organization. Lost Art participated in Gen Art's catwalk shows in 1998 and 2000; at the latter Betten won the menswear designer award.

Lost Art uses soft, supple skins for its precisely seamed leather offerings such as snug-fitting leather trousers, snakeskin coats and fringed suede shawls as well as other accessories. Betten's clientele includes a number of rock and country-and-western musicians who wear his designs both on and off the stage. Betten's leather creations appeal to other clients who may see the clothes as a means of associating themselves with the glamour of rock-and-roll leathers. But surely what most of his clients come to Betten for is a handcrafted garment. As fashion curator Andrew Bolton suggests, 'In this era of techno textiles the use of complete animal hides by couturiers is an assertion of authenticity.'[2] Betten agreed, stating, 'People buy Lost Art because they're looking for an original piece with well-made, quality details.'[3]

Betten's leather trousers epitomize his craft. Each pair is unique, made from a specifically chosen skin. The most basic pair of suede or leather trousers takes Betten and his studio at least four full days to make. First he measures the client and then together they discuss the type of materials and trimmings to be used. Not until then does Betten purchase the leather. For clients who are not a standard size, next Betten makes the muslin toile he uses to test the fit before the leather is cut. A fitting for the client follows, after which he makes a pattern for the garment (he will save the pattern in case the client comes back for further pairs). He then cuts the leather (Lost Art does not use machines), and adds any embellishments such as feathers or contrasting skins onto the surface. The trousers are then made up by lacing the seams closed through the hundreds of small holes Betten has punched along the seam lines. For laces Betten uses thin strips of the same leather as the trousers. Such individual client attention and the deliberate pace of the design process means that the scale of Betten's business is small. Not counting some of the larger orders for high-profile musicians, the studio creates just over one hundred garments per year. The prices reflect this labour-intensive, artisanal approach:

ABOVE Lost Art by Jordan Betten, woven leather trousers with fringe, 2002. Photo: Colin Fitzpatrick.

OPPOSITE Lost Art by Jordan Betten, deer suede suit, 2003. Photo: Natalie Czartoryski.

a pair of Lost Art leather trousers starts at $2,500 but extravagant creations can cost as much as $40,000 for an intricately woven leather version (opposite).

Betten's prominent musician-clients include Willie Nelson, Lenny Kravitz, Britney Spears and Sheryl Crow (see p.107). Their patronage suggests that Lost Art deserves discussion in the context of fashion and celebrity. Although Betten's performance pieces are dramatic and arresting, he makes them with the same care and techniques as the clothes he makes for everyday wear. That Betten designs for both stage and street shows a rare breadth of range: costumier as well as traditional craftsman.

We don't use sewing machines so every piece is completely handmade. Everything is one-of-a-kind and custom-made for the person who's going to be wearing it.[+]

Lost Art by Jordan Betten, cheetah trimmed trousers with snakeskin shawl, 2004–5. Photo: Marco Guerra.

Further evidence of Betten's skill as a designer and technician is his handling of colour and texture, and the range of materials he uses with such assurance. Assisted by his colleague Jun Funahashi, Betten turned a quasi-shamanistic shawl into a kinetic sculpture by trimming a soft, mottled coyote pelt with feathers and a wispy, tan rattlesnake skin fringe (opposite). In this ensemble Betten accented the trouser cuffs with cheetah fur. Completing the look is a thick, grey badger fur hat. The outfit exemplifies Lost Art's combination of the exotic (cheetah and snakeskin trimming) with the erotic (in the form of skin-tight leather). The atelier reinforces this exotic/erotic formula in its press material and website, which feature provocative photographs of semi-clothed models in body-clinging leather creations.

Lost Art's materials are central to Betten's designs. Betten sources most of his leathers by the square foot. He chooses hides individually, purchasing only enough at a time (35 feet or so) for a single pair of trousers – in marked contrast to standard manufacturers who may buy several thousand square feet at a time. Because each Lost Art project is unique, Betten purchases with particular care, selecting skin specifically for each garment. For him, the colour and texture of the material dictate the form the design will take. The hides Betten chooses are pre-tanned, ensuring that colours and textures are as he wishes. Betten then carries out his own surface treatments. For example, to create a patina of age Betten adds more oils to the leather or distresses it with sandpaper.

Lost Art's deer suede woman's trouser suit is a further illustration of Betten's focused attention on materials (see p.057). Like a traditional man's three-piece suit, this ensemble – adapted from one of Lost Art's male patterns – consists of trousers, waistcoat and jacket. But the soft luxury of suede moves it very far from the realm of the traditional or conservative uniform. For the prototype, Betten used 18 deer hides, all carefully matched for colour and texture so that they appeared to be from the same animal. Betten finished the seams of all three components with criss-cross leather lacing, lending a tactile, three-dimensional quality to the surface. Plaited strips of the same leather composed the jacket buttons. The trousers lace up over leather gussets at both hips, a construction technique ensuring precise fit while allowing the wearer freedom of movement. The visible precision of Lost Art's stitching and lacing demonstrate Betten's mastery of intricate construction techniques for a material that is very difficult to manipulate.

Viewing himself as a conservationist, Betten recognizes a possible perception of moral ambiguity in his use of animal skins for adornment. His conservationism, he explains, is akin to recycling: pelts of endangered species in Lost Art's garments always come from pre-existing cast-offs, found at vintage or antique markets. Betten said, 'I'm a strong believer in conservation and animal treatment and I think that's a big part of what we do, actually, that we're celebrating the material. Each skin dictates what we make from it. It's almost as if I'm trying to channel the spirit of that animal. Hopefully, when we've finish working with it, it's almost proud to look down.'

JEAN YU

OPPOSITE ABOVE Jean Yu, dress worn by
Gwen Stefani, 2004. Photo: © Steven
Meisel/Art + Commerce, originally
published in *Vogue*.

BELOW LEFT Jean Yu, underpants, 2002.
Photo: Robin Broadbent.

BELOW RIGHT Jean Yu, garter, 2002.
Photo: Robin Broadbent.

While materials preoccupy Jordan Betten, Jean Yu (b. 1968) focuses on precise cut
and meticulous construction. The Korean-born, New York-based Yu makes carefully
crafted dresses, separates and lingerie with finishing techniques such as hand-rolled
hems and French seams. Yu uses fine, translucent silks, chiffons and jerseys, in
a palette of black, white and the occasional splash of colour. She sells out of her
SoHo shop, which she named 'Atelier=37', and creates many of the garments,
both ready-to-wear and bespoke, in the basement workshop below. After studying
fashion design at FIT and a number of years spent designing an anonymous high-
end fashion line for specialty department stores, Yu started her business in order to
achieve design freedom and to sell directly to clients. Using the atelier model of a
small shop connected to a design studio has allowed the designer to build a business
slowly without financial backers, while monitoring quality and craftsmanship.

Jean Yu opened Atelier=37 in December 2001 during the confused, desperate
period after the September 11 terrorist attacks. With her shop's location less than
two miles from the World Trade Center, Yu struggled, along with many other shops
and businesses in her area. The designer's recollections of that period are evocative:

For the first two years I think I cried almost every day. I thought I made the biggest mistake.[5]

While some of her neighbours eventually closed their businesses, Yu persevered
and built a loyal clientele. A turning-point for the designer was *Vogue's* April 2004
front cover that featured Gwen Stefani wearing one of Yu's designs (opposite,
above). The following year, as one of ten finalists for the 2005 CFDA/*Vogue* Fund,
Yu was accorded a double-page spread in the magazine's November write-up of
the contest. *Vogue* editorial described Yu's clothes as 'simple yet sumptuous'.

Yu acknowledges that broad recognition plays an important part in a
designer's career, but she said of the CFDA/*Vogue* experience, 'I haven't seen it
impact my business concretely.' The exposure did encourage Yu to launch annual
collections, however, beginning with the Spring/Summer 2005 season. She now
designs two collections a year, each containing around two dozen different dress
styles in addition to her lingerie designs. Instead of staging catwalk presentations
Yu schedules appointments in her atelier to introduce the clothes to retailers.
Although her business has grown, it still operates on a small scale: she sells via
stores in New York, Miami and Los Angeles as well as Celux, the Louis Vuitton
Moët Hennessy members-only salon in Tokyo, and London's Harvey Nichols and
Dover Street Market.

Yu's concern with precision leads her to prefer designing in black-and-white
to emphasize the linear, architectural quality of her work. Within this limited
palette, she builds up different levels of opacity by layering her sheer chiffon,
resulting in variety and vitality. According to Yu, the lightweight quality of the
materials she uses renders them seasonless, and the graphic linearity of her designs
makes them appropriate for many different settings and situations. She stated:

Each piece is conceived as a pure, complete and enduring example of design in its essence.[6]

Yu's black chiffon garter and white chiffon underpants with black waistband
illustrate her color preference, high level of detail and her layered opacity (opposite,
below). A white chiffon dress (see p.051) with back drape and waistband from

Jean Yu, chiffon dress, Spring/Summer 2006. Photo: Kenny Jossick.

her Spring/Summer 2006 collection has no seams, and is cut from a single piece of cloth. She explains that the dress starts out as a perfect square. The square is folded on the diagonal to bring together the two opposite corners, which meet at centre back, thus generating the flow of the bias drapes and says Yu, 'From one point to the other, the soft rolled hem routes its course in a continuum.'

Yu describes herself as both cautious and controlling. Operating without a business partner or a press relations representative, she does the work herself, carefully vetting press requests to photograph her clothes and choosing the stores that will carry her designs. Her own boutique is far from a traditional retail environment and suggests how she wishes her work to be perceived. The atelier is a narrow sliver, its main feature a gallery-like white wall displaying Yu's designs.

Although Yu makes all the business decisions, her primary concern as a designer is construction: 'My garments are architectural. I'm obsessed with their construction. For me, that is the focal point.' However, in contrast to the designs of her atelier contemporary Jordan Betten, she believes that her creations do not depend on hand-sewing to succeed. For Yu, the crucial element in achieving her graphic, architectural silhouettes is precision, and this means sewing with machines.

While Yu manufactures some pieces at a few small local factories, she makes the majority of her designs in the atelier, sitting with her sewers while they construct the made-to-measure garments. She has offered this bespoke service, along with her ready-to-wear designs, since she opened her doors. The designer sees her bespoke work as a personal indulgence. She enjoys the intimacy of the designer/client exchange, and the process of taking measurements, making a toile or pattern, overseeing the fittings and then constructing the garment. With this meticulous made-to-measure service, a shop connected to a design studio and the creative freedom she once craved, Yu has created her ideal of an atelier business model. While she acknowledges the pressure of New York's fashion culture to make 'bankable, safer clothes', as an independent designer without a financial backer to satisfy, it is a pressure that Yu – like her atelier contemporaries – has thus far evaded.

MAGGIE NORRIS

Of the four featured atelier designers, Maggie Norris had the most industry experience before she started out on her own, having worked for 14 years at Ralph Lauren. Her last position at the company was Senior Design Director for womenswear. Norris launched her couture-centred eponymous line in the autumn of 2000 with a salon-style fashion show at Bergdorf Goodman. Like Betten and Yu, she sells made-to-measure garments out of an atelier-like space with a workshop attached. She is, like them, wholly preoccupied with the details of her craft. Her tailored daywear and elegant eveningwear feature rarefied construction techniques along with occasional historic references and vintage textiles. A high standard of craftsmanship and the use of luxurious textiles set her clothes apart.

Norris left Ralph Lauren intending to design couture-level clothes – meaning not only clothes made-to-measure but also garments harnessing the technical skills of talented craftspeople such as cutters, seamstresses and embroiderers. Before starting out on her own, Norris spent a year researching resources and suppliers. It was, according to the designer, a year of wondrous excitement. Norris' research was centred on realizing her first collection, an equestrian-inspired group of garments for which she tracked down some of the best makers in the business. Her investigations took her to London's august Savile Row and New Bond Street where she commissioned some of London's top bespoke houses to create specific elements of the collection. She enlisted Kilgour to custom-make her jodhpurs, Lock and Co. hatters to make nineteenth-century-inspired dressage hats and Schnieder to create hand-crafted equestrian boots. All these businesses are specialists in their metier; Schnieder possesses the Royal Warrant and supplies boots to the Queen's Household Cavalry.

The high cost of Norris' labour-intensive designs (an evening gown starts at $8,000 and can reach $50,000 depending on fabric, embroidery, corsetry and other factors) comes with high client expectations. While Norris continues to travel abroad to visit European suppliers and design specialists such as the Parisian embroidery firm Lesage, she must remain available for her clients. Norris clearly enjoys this aspect of her work. She explained, 'New York is the fashion place to be. [My] clients are well-travelled; they're in New York, Los Angeles and Palm Beach.' She added:

Each client represents a whole set of intricacies in pleasing her and making her look beautiful.[7]

Her clients' expectations for carefully constructed, luxurious bespoke designs are realized in part through the work of the half dozen skilled craftspeople Norris employs. Norris possesses a reverence for their skills, saying, 'I respect the craft'. She also sees her workshop as a refuge for them. 'They need me, in the sense that they couldn't go and work for Tommy [Hilfiger]. With [production] going offshore, to China, they need work.'

While Norris' first few collections were entirely couture, she later experimented briefly with ready-to-wear. However, she asserts that designing ready-to-wear brings compromise. 'It changes everything,' she said. While her ready-to-wear experiment lasted, in her words, 'about one minute', Norris does now offer pre-made, sized shirts, which she feels she can semi-standardize without conceding quality. But this brush with ready-to-wear seems to have reaffirmed Norris' devotion to high craft. While she admitted to missing the support and resources of a large organization, she countered that 'the rewards are so tremendous'.

TOP Maggie Norris, corset top and embroidered skirt, 2003. Photo: David Ferrura, originally published in *Elegant Bride*.

ABOVE Maggie Norris, linen corset top, 2001. Photo: Ruven Afanador, originally published in *Elle*.

OPPOSITE Maggie Norris, sleeve detail, 2001. Photo: Marlene Weatherall.

Design freedom is clearly a benefit of Norris' entrepreneurial venture. She particularly enjoys working with antique textiles, even fragments, which she occasionally incorporates into her designs. She also seeks out collaborations with outside craftspeople, such as the French makers and London specialists previously mentioned. The designer is busy enough to be reluctant to take on new clients. She has established a couture salon within Bergdorf Goodman, in addition to selling out of her design premises. Maggie Norris' atelier has thrived, in the view of its founder, by 'word of mouth, a striving for perfection and refusal to give up on [my] ideals', a formula that could also apply to all four atelier designers mentioned in this chapter.

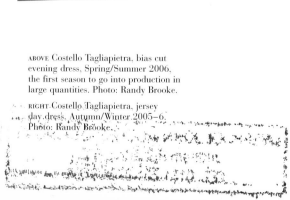

ABOVE Costello Tagliapietra, bias cut
evening dress, Spring/Summer 2006,
the first season to go into production in
large quantities. Photo: Randy Brooke.

RIGHT Costello Tagliapietra, jersey
day dress, Autumn/Winter 2005–6.
Photo: Randy Brooke.

COSTELLO TAGLIAPIETRA

Jeffrey Costello and Robert Tagliapietra's eponymous design label, founded in 2003, is the newest of the four atelier examples. The duo established their textile-focused womenswear line after a number of years spent designing stage clothes and bespoke ensembles for private clients such as Bruce Springsteen, Madonna and members of the band Depeche Mode. Basing their design studio in their shared Brooklyn apartment, they spent several years building their new business and private clientele through custom, made-to-measure designs.

Costello (b. 1962) and Tagliapietra (b. 1974) share every aspect of running their business, from managing the finances to designing the clothes. Their design aim is to bring back the pleasure of small details to women's clothing. To achieve this, they incorporate time-consuming dressmaking features such as rolled edges, old-fashioned interior belts, and zips with vintage lace trim. The designers also ensure that strips of bias-cut silk organza are laid down and pressed onto most of their seams, resulting in both a cleaner, purer line and a stronger construction. Such details, which the designers refer to as the 'treats inside', are made all the more noticeable in Costello Tagliapietra's collections by the complete absence of the distractions of surface pattern and applied embellishment. Precise cut and lack of ornament result in pared-down silhouettes that celebrate a minimal aesthetic.

Perhaps even more crucial to Costello Tagliapietra's designs than the hidden luxuries of their construction are the fabrics, most often single- or double-knit jersey. When Jeffrey Costello talks about this fabric's possibilities, his enthusiasm is evident. 'Jersey does everything we need. It can create both a fluid, draped piece and… more form-fitting garments. Boiled or felted, it becomes tightened or thickened but it retains the flexibility of a knit.'[8] The designers view this fabric as crucial to their collections.

Initially, Costello and Tagliapietra sold their clothing exclusively out of their Brooklyn design studio. Many of their clothes were made-to-measure for each customer, enabling the designers to adjust the garment according to a client's taste and figure. They view this early involvement with individual garment quality as a step towards helping them build their label's reputation, resulting in early acknowledgement and praise from retailers and the fashion press.

In 2005, Costello Tagliapietra won broader recognition and underwent a change of business strategy. The company was one of six to win the Ecco Domani Fashion Foundation award, and one of ten finalists in the 2005 CFDA/*Vogue* Fashion Fund. They later commented: 'It helped us because we're a young company. It's nice to get that respect and acknowledgement.' Alongside the increased visibility came an interest from retailers in Costello Tagliapietra designs. By the end of the year their clothes were available in a handful of shops in New York, Paris and Los Angeles.[9]

In order to produce the garment quantities needed to fill these retailers' orders, Costello and Tagliapietra required manufacturing assistance and began the difficult search for factories. Insisting on local production in order to monitor quality more easily, the quest, which the designers described as 'next to impossible', took time. They eventually started working with two Manhattan-based firms (one is a factory, in business since the 1950s, that has produced garments for the likes of Geoffrey Beene and Oscar de la Renta). The factories Costello and Tagliapietra work with are, like their remaining local competitors, willing to produce the emerging design label's relatively modest quantities – for Costello Tagliapietra, typically around 60 pieces of a single style. They are clear about their relationship with factories and the challenge of outsourcing production.

LIVERPOOL JOHN MOORES UNIVERSITY
Aldham Roberts L.R.C.
TEL 0151 231 3701/3634

We don't compromise in our work. We can't because we have a lot to lose, since we're so small.

Initially, to avoid conflicting with the retailers selling their designs, Jeffrey Costello and Robert Tagliapietra have discontinued their studio-based bespoke service. They hope to reinstate it once their retail customer is established. Their aim in selling through established retail outlets is, as any designer might profess, to produce and sell in larger quantities while maintaining the integrity of their designs. The designers clearly believe that the secret to maintaining this balance lies in the expertise of the factories they work with.

Costello and Tagliapietra speak with deep admiration about the technical abilities of their manufacturing partners. A dress from Autumn/Winter 2006–7 that is, according to the designers, particularly difficult to produce, illustrates New York's high level of manufacturing skill. Made from panels of delicate, bias-cut silk chiffon, the dress's bodice is gathered at the neck and waist, while the back is slit and falls open in a delicate drape (opposite). According to Jeffrey Costello, a further example of factory quality is that the seamstresses forgo the ease of an overlock machine in favour of more old-fashioned single needle machines for seamwork. While both factories *have* an overlock machine, said Costello, 'When I go to visit, usually I see it being used as a lunch table.' He continued, 'I view this as a mark of quality. You're getting a more luxurious, better-made garment.'

Designers who start labels adhering to the atelier model – a preoccupation with fabrics, cut and construction – tend to have only limited distribution. Lost Art, Jean Yu and Maggie Norris sell out of their ateliers and to a few select stores. Costello Tagliapietra, in outsourcing their production to highly skilled local factories and actively seeking to expand their business internationally, are at an important juncture for their fledgling label. Such attempts to balance the creative delights of high craft with manufactured production (particularly that of talented and local factories) may be the secret strength of New York fashion's future.

Costello Tagliapietra, silk day dress, Autumn/Winter 2006–7. Photo: Randy Brooke.

AVANT-GARDE

As Four. 'Human Plant'. 1998. Rubber.
Photo: courtesy of Three As Four.

AVANT-GARDE
SUBVERSIVE STATEMENTS

Miguel Adrover, Burberry coat-dress, Autumn/Winter 2000–1. Photo: catwalking.com.

New York's reputation for producing saleable, commercial clothes perpetuates a fashion culture that values practicality, quality and comfort. Such commercialism makes New York a challenging city for designers with more radical aspirations. Does New York fashion (or any fashion, for that matter) with its concern for pragmatism and profit merit the label 'avant-garde'? Academic Peter Bürger defined the intention of the historical avant-garde movements as 'the destruction of art as an institution', and their significance as the fundamental change they made to 'the place of political engagement in art'.[1] It seems incongruous to apply the nihilist intent of this conception of the avant-garde and its powerful influence to the vagaries of the fashion world. A more inclusive definition of the avant-garde would account for fashion's rebel spirits whose aim would be to change rather than to destroy. Fashion curator Claire Wilcox's characterization of fashion outside the mainstream serves this purpose. She writes that such fashion '…is really about pushing boundaries, challenging preconceptions, exceeding limitations and ultimately finding a balance between conformity and eccentricity, function and adornment.'[2]

Paris, Tokyo, London and Antwerp have all produced acclaimed twentieth-century fashion iconoclasts. These cities' strong traditions of avant-gardist fashion accommodate and even celebrate the unorthodox. In contrast, most New York-based designers who have prospered in the past have done so by avoiding radical cut or aberrant construction. However, in spite of the continued importance of New York's mainstream ready-to-wear and sportswear, a handful of designers have challenged the constraints of America's commercially based fashion industry. Although the avant-gardists operate within the fashion system – presenting their collections during New York Fashion Week and selling their clothes via established retailers – these designers see themselves as fashion outsiders.

Is it a contradiction in terms to design subversive fashion within the boundaries of function and commerce? The creations of the New York avant-gardists Slow and Steady Wins the Race, Tess Giberson, Three As Four and Miguel Adrover are records of attempts to do both. These four labels are rare examples of contemporary New York fashion designed in opposition to the mainstream. Several features characterize their approaches. They explore unusual construction and silhouettes. They may also design according to a utopian manifesto. The designers make clothes that embody a narrative or historical reference. Further, three of them have experimented with different methods of presenting their work. Two of these four designers started designing in their early to mid-20s and came from abroad, bringing an outsider's perspective to their metier.

SLOW AND STEADY
WINS THE RACE

ABOVE Slow and Steady Wins the Race,
reinterpretation of Gucci handbag,
'Bags' collection, 2002.

OPPOSITE Slow and Steady Wins the
Race, hang tag with manifesto, 2002.

Founding her conceptual clothing line in 2001 at 23, the creator of Slow and Steady Wins the Race (Slow and Steady) was the youngest of the avant-gardists to launch her own label. The designer, who creates the line anonymously, began with little formal fashion training. After receiving a BA in fine art, she began designing fashions according to an anti-consumerist manifesto; she intends these collections, up to four a year, to slow the pace of fashion's built-in obsolescence. The designer aims to, in her words, 'produce interesting and significant pieces from the most inexpensive fabrics and materials.'[3] She describes her intent as 'concept-driven', with each collection 'based on a design fundamental' ranging from the status handbag to the essentials of eveningwear.[4] The designer, who sells her clothes via boutiques in New York, Los Angeles and Tokyo, makes a large number of the pieces herself, thus saving on production costs. The saving is passed on to the client in order to promote what she calls 'a democratic and grass-roots distribution' of good design. Slow and Steady's initial manifesto pledged that each piece would cost under $100 and would be made in a limited edition of 100.

Slow and Steady's designer wants to create clothes that minimize the waste of the fashion cycle. She elaborated:

I thought a lot about the mechanics of the trade – the sheer volume of clothing that is produced. Before starting the label, I came across a *New York Times* article tracing the life of a T shirt… from a local charity shop… through many rounds of garment collection and redistribution to poorer, third-world nations until it ended up being sold at a market in Ghana for what was the U.S. equivalent of a fraction of a penny. It cemented my idea that good design could be addressed in moderation since it should be able to exist for years to come.[5]

Since then the designer has investigated a number of themes. 'Seams', the label's first collection, consisted of six pieces: a jacket, skirt, two T-shirts, a tank top and a bag. The garments were all made from plain cotton canvas with the seams, normally hidden inside, deliberately made visible (see pp.076–7). She explained her intention: 'In this first collection I wanted to show how clothes are put together… the six pieces were very basic silhouettes, used really simple material and the seams were all worked on the outside.' Each garment was ticketed with an envelope containing an explanatory missive to the purchaser. It cautioned, 'With each passing year, new faces and new ideas pop into existence, which in turn sprout, float and germinate into more categorical stuff. As a result, a decided amount is kept and a more considerable amount is laid to waste.'

With collections such as Seams, Slow and Steady's designer follows in a long tradition of experimenting with humble materials to create fashionable clothing. From Chanel's first jersey garments in the 1910s to Martin Margiela's use of recycled garments to make high fashion offerings in the 1990s, showing functionality in fashion design is nothing new. A distinctive element of Slow and Steady's 'Seams' collection is that the designer severely limited its production and its price: only 100 pieces of each style were made and all were priced under $100. Through these limits, the designer aimed to make good design affordable but not cheapened by mass-distribution.

While Seams promoted a capsule wardrobe, other Slow and Steady collections were meditations on a single garment: the label's third series, entitled 'Bags', deconstructed the designer handbag. The designer presented six stripped-down interpretations of popular purses such as the Hermès Birkin Bag, the Gucci bamboo-handled bag and Chanel's quilted leather bag with gold chain strap. Keeping these bags' basic shapes and retaining a few recognizable features such as fastenings or textile treatments, she produced the styles in plain cotton canvas. The reinterpreted Gucci bag kept the original's bamboo hardware, quilted surface and Gucci-specific green and red grosgrain ribbon (opposite). Slow and Steady's plain canvas version, like a ghostly reference to the original's luxury, further dramatized the celebrity achieved by the mere shape of the high-status bag. In the words of the designer, through this process, the status bag becomes 'an alternate icon of itself'.[6]

But Bags made the designer recognize the tension between her manifesto and the need for financial stability. Her canvas reinterpretation of Balenciaga's 2003 motorcycle saddle bag was so popular, thanks to its brief appearance on the American television series *Sex and the City*, that many hundreds of orders came in for the one style. In violation of her original manifesto, the designer decided to honour the orders. This experience convinced her to change Slow and Steady's original philosophy. The financial pressures of being a young designer in New York brought the realization that it was not economically sound to limit each design to 100 pieces. Slow and Steady's revised limit is 3,500 units, a quantity the designer thinks allows for profit while still avoiding market saturation.

Although a life-long New Yorker, like other avant-gardists the Slow and Steady creator thinks of herself as a New York fashion outsider. She commented, 'I think of New York design as sportswear and street fashion... Paris is a city still fostering a creative sensibility. So I wonder what it would be like designing in Paris?' The designer reflected on the difficulties of young entrepreneurialism by saying, 'In New York, if you're *really* young you can make it only so far through hype and some talent. But these designers can blow up or just disappear. And often the ones who are still hanging on... lose their creativity.'

Slow and Steady Wins the Race
Nº3 'The Bag'
Gucci Bag

Slow and Steady Wins the Race
www.slowandsteadywinstherace.com
slowandsteady2002@hotmail.com

Slow and Steady Wins the Race
Nº3 'The Bag'

The third issue of Slow and Steady Wins the Race is about...

Slow and Steady Wins the Race,
cotton canvas suit with T-shirt, 'Seams'
collection, Spring/Summer 2001.
Loan: Slow and Steady Wins the Race.

TESS GIBERSON

Like the collections of Slow and Steady Wins the Race, Tess Giberson's carefully considered, poetic collections each start with an intellectual preoccupation. While Slow and Steady's designer creates according to an economic manifesto, Giberson (b. 1971) designs around central themes ranging from individual and community shelter to story-telling. Giberson grew up in an artistic household (her mother and father are artists) and is a graduate of Rhode Island School of Design with a BFA in apparel design. Her first collection (Spring/Summer 2002) was a small group of one-of-a-kind pieces sold via New York's influential fashion boutique Seven.

While inspired by the city's vibrancy, Giberson, like the SSWTR creator, is ambivalent about New York as a base for designing and marketing clothes that are more conceptual than commercial. She said:

I love New York and living in New York… but I don't think it really affects the aesthetic of my work because I don't consider myself an American designer – people don't usually know that I'm American from my work. There are a lot of frustrations with showing in New York because it's very, very commercial, and what's accepted as fashion is a very narrow category… in Paris, they're much more open. The same people can see your show in Paris and New York and they'll criticize it in New York, where they would love it in Paris. I'd love to show in Paris.[7]

Like Slow and Steady's creator, Giberson criticized New York's fickle support of young designers, faulting the cyclical search for the next fresh design face. 'It's very supportive for the first two seasons, but then it's not supportive of developing the business… it's great when you get the initial hype, the initial energy, but there is no support set up for what comes next and how to really build your business. So you've got either very young designers or much more established designers, and there is a real gap in between.' However, Giberson admitted, 'I have a really supportive following… clients who have been buying my clothes since the beginning.' In addition to praising her loyal clientele, Giberson admires the skills of local manufacturers. She has worked with a New York-area factory to produce most of her designs. For Giberson, having the factory nearby ensures quality control. 'If there is a problem, I just go down. It's so much easier than flying to either Europe or Asia. Also, I like the idea of working domestically.'

One source of support for Giberson's business came from the Ecco Domani Fashion Foundation, for in 2002 she entered and won the annual EDFF competition. The award financed Giberson's catwalk show during New York Fashion Week and helped her to stage a presentation that was an extension of her lyrical design vision. Giberson has always preferred formats that are markedly different from traditional catwalk shows. The presentation of her Autumn/Winter 2003–4 collection, entitled 'Structure No. 1', explored the idea of individual community

collection, entitled 'Structure No. 1', explored the idea of individual community and shelter. Working with a dancer to choreograph the models, Giberson instructed them to use her embellished skirts, tailored jackets and prim dresses to create a temporary shelter in front of the audience. The designer showcased the event at the Le Tea Theater in the Lower East Side. The models disrobed down to plain white slips and then placed Giberson's designs on a temporary pole-studded structure. The last model enclosed the entire clothing-strewn arrangement by winding a length of plain white fabric around it, thus creating a shelter into which all the models then entered (see p.080–081). Giberson explained her intention: 'I started thinking about what made up a community in which all the individuals have to work together and need some kind of shelter structure.'

Giberson's intellectual approach to fashion has attracted the attention of the international arts community. In 2002 New York's Cooper-Hewitt National Design Museum hosted the National Design Triennial Conference, during which it installed Structure No. 1 and included a video presentation of the original fashion show. Giberson's narrative collections found an enthusiastic audience in Japan; when the designer was most active, seven Japanese stores stocked her work (double the number in America). Giberson displayed her designs in Tokyo's Laforet Museum and at the Taka Ishii Gallery.

Tess Giberson, collection
Autumn/Winter 2005-6.
Photo: Yangton.

BELOW LEFT Tess Giberson for TSE, cashmere scoop neck sweater with exaggerated trousers, Spring/Summer 2007. Photo: Monica Freudi.

BELOW RIGHT AND OPPOSITE Tess Giberson, Structure #1, Autumn/Winter 2003–4. Photos: Jonah Freeman.

Although staged, choreographed presentations served Giberson's art-based conception of fashion, they made it difficult for some buyers and members of the press to understand and appreciate the clothes. Perhaps in acknowledgement of this, Giberson presented her 2005 collections in a manner closer to traditional catwalk shows. In contrast to her more narrative presentations, for the Spring/Summer 2005 collection Giberson still investigated an idea or theme, but showed her clothes on models who walked back and forth in front of the audience. For this season Giberson created a series of designs whose form went from structured to billowing ethereality, and whose colour developed from white to grey. The concept that Giberson investigated in this Spring/Summer 2005 collection was the ambiguity of a shadow, that it is both real and not real.[8] Giberson also presented Autumn/Winter 2005–6 on the catwalk. For this collection Giberson, who was pregnant at the time, explored the theme of magnification: she noticeably enlarged the pockets, collars, sleeves, waistbands, tucks and pleats of otherwise straightforward garments. This exaggeration drew attention to the garments and encouraged the viewer look more closely at the clothes. Giberson cares deeply that these collections have transcended trends. She said, 'I don't design a trend for the season that you can't ever wear again. It's nice to see how things age, how they actually grow.'

After five years of designing her own label, in late 2005 Giberson was approached by the luxury knitwear label TSE to be its head designer. For Giberson, designing both collections simultaneously, on top of recent motherhood would have been unrealistic. Thus Giberson decided to close down her label and take her talents to TSE.

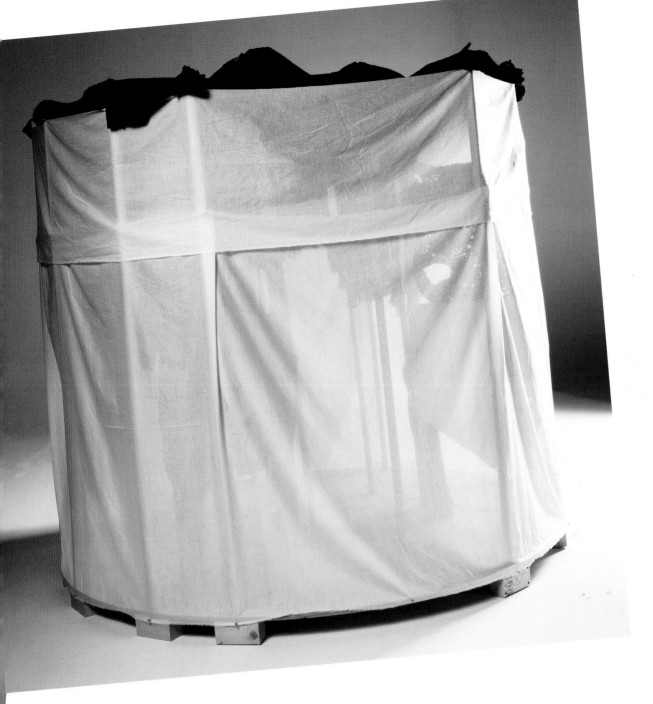

THREE AS FOUR

Like Slow and Steady Wins the Race, the avant-garde design-label Three As Four is focused on both the final products and the ideas behind them. Three As Four's designs assume that their ideal client is an urban individualist who appreciates unusual cut and offbeat silhouettes and who enjoys, even courts, notice. The trio began in 1998 as a foursome known as As Four. The two male designers were Kai and Gabi; the two women Ange and Adi. When Kai left in 2005 to design his own clothing line, the three continued, amending their label name. The design collective is an international mix: Gabi (b. 1966) is a Lebanese-born Palestinian, Adi (b. 1971) is Israeli and Ange (b. 1974) is from Tajikistan.

Before starting the label, Gabi worked for mainstream fashion companies such as DKNY, Marc Jacobs and Kate Spade. Ange and Adi met at design school in Germany. The two women moved to New York in the early 1990s, spent several years working together as fashion stylists, then met their male design partners several years later. After launching in 1998 As Four made their runway debut in 2001, and with their first designs they demonstrated a profound concern with unexpected cut and construction. From their silver-painted Chinatown loft (see pp.018–19), Three As Four design clothes whose asymmetrical cut and curved seams result in silhouettes that swirl and blossom around the body. The designers described their patterns as 'so crazy, that you need somebody that's very close to you to really understand.'[9] In order to secure a reliable means of producing these patterns, the designers encouraged a relative of Gabi's to open a garment factory.

A 1998 design, 'Human Plant', showcased their virtuoso construction techniques. Inspired by the hard shells of crustaceans such as shrimp, the unitard-like suit is composed entirely of concentric rubber circles stitched onto a mesh backing (p.071 and opposite). The design is complex, yet the wearer's body moves gracefully inside. Gabi explained:

The first thing we did was tack together one continuing shape… playing around with this whole idea of skin and bones. With humans and mammals there's skin over bones so your movement is soft over hard. In insects you have soft inside and hard outside, as with crabs and shrimp. They move in a whole different way.

Although Three As Four have showed their designs on the Fashion Week catwalks, like their avant-garde colleagues they have also experimented with different methods of presentation. In 2000 Kim Hastreiter, the co-editor of fashion's independent-minded *Paper* magazine, invited the foursome to stage an unorthodox fashion presentation during New York Fashion week at the Bryant Park tents. For the event, which they dubbed 'Puppencouture' (opposite), the designers dressed scores of small-scale, wind-up fashion dolls in their designs. They then unleashed the dolls to careen randomly across the stage, sometimes bumping into each other and toppling over as Wagner was played in the background. The experience was repeated in Paris at the Purple Institute and then at the Septième Étage Gallery in Geneva. As Four later sized up some of these miniature garments and put them into production.

As Four revisited this small-scale theme in the catwalk presentation of their Autumn/Winter 2004 collection. The designers used children to model clothes that, with their petal-shaped appliqués and sparkling fabrics, were fairy-like in inspiration. These fanciful designs contrasted with the 13 severe, all-black ensembles in the same collection modelled by the adults on stage. The proceedings featured additional stimuli: a puppet-show performance and a soundtrack that included a tinkling composition that resembled the tune of a musical box.

Staying in business since 1998 and continuing to sell their clothes in some of the world's most prestigious retailers, by many measures the trio have done well. Still, their clothes appeal to a very select audience and they have struggled financially. In an attempt to create an additional clothing line with more commercial appeal, they devised a denim series integrating Three As Four's signature curved seams, petal shapes and cocoon-like silhouettes (see pp.084–85). They launched the line in 2005 with ensembles that included trousers, tops, shorts and jackets along with evening dresses of crumpled, layered or net-like denim. The denim garments are less expensive than Three As Four's signature collection since it is hoped that the new line will net them a broader clientele. In this aim they are similar to another fashion label, Imitation of Christ (IOC), who added a denim line to their main label in Spring/Summer 2006. IOC received early notoriety from their incorporation of flea-market finds and reused vintage clothing, as well as from their unorthodox fashion show presentations in venues such as a funeral parlour and a circus. But while IOC softened their anti-establishment stance, Three As Four's designs have maintained a subversive edge.

Although Three As Four show during Fashion Week, sell their clothes internationally and design a slightly more commercial denim line, they see themselves as struggling outsiders. Ange commented, 'We get a lot of non-response from Europe because we're here. They think that anybody that is from New York is not good enough. But we feel that we're as good as the Europeans.' Echoing the theme of displacement, Gabi declared: 'There's a major decay of culture… a whole young generation that is falling apart. We're living in a time of decay and (New York) is the place that you feel it the most. I think in terms of what we do it's not the place to be. We should be in Paris.'

Yet each of the Three As Four designers came to the United States and to New York specifically because it is where they dreamt of living and working; it is the city where they 'want to make it'. They enjoy designing for a devoted group of fashion loyalists. Equally significant, they embrace, are inspired by and indeed exemplify their adopted city's cosmopolitan mix.

OPPOSITE Three As Four, children wearing garments from Autumn/Winter 2004–05. Photo: courtesy of Three As Four.

ABOVE LEFT As Four, 'Human Plant', 1998. Rubber. Photo: courtesy of As Four.

ABOVE RIGHT As Four, a design for 'Puppencouture', 2000. Photo: courtesy of As Four.

Three As Four. denim designs.
Spring/Summer 2005.
Photo: Marcelo Krasilcic.

MIGUEL ADROVER

Like Gabi, Ange and Adi of Three As Four, the Majorcan designer Miguel Adrover (b. 1965) created his clothes as a New York-based émigré. More than his fellow avant-gardists, Adrover's fashion career illustrates the difficulties of expressing a radical design sensibility in New York. The closure of his five-year-old fashion label in 2005 and his subsequent abandonment of the New York fashion industry serve as a stark reminder of the challenges faced by emerging designers, and particularly those expressing an unconventional point of view.

Adrover arrived in New York in 1991 at the age of 26 with no formal design training. He began by making customized T-shirts with his friend Douglas Hobbs. In 1995 the pair opened Horn, an East Village boutique selling the creations of other experimental designers, along with their own. Four years later, Adrover started his own label. He recognized at the time that New York was not historically hospitable to those outside the mainstream. 'There was very little attention given in New York to avant-garde designers – it [wasn't] something that the city's fashion industry [was] open to. But it was a moment when the city was open to new things.'[10]

Adrover presented his first solo collection, entitled 'Manaus-Chiapas' (Spring/Summer 2000), in 1999. This collection established Adrover's reputation for a fine sense of cut and construction, as well as his interest in found objects and recycled clothing. Manaus-Chiapas set a precedent for Adrover's provocative, politically themed collections that often spanned the divide between the commercial and the avant-garde.

Manaus-Chiapas chronicled the story of a woman forced out of her Brazilian rainforest home, fleeing to Mexico, and then to New York. Motivating the collection, Adrover said, was the petrol companies' destructive industrialization of the Manaus jungles as well as conflicts between the Chiapas people and the Mexican government. Adrover represented the refugee's arrival in New York through his clothes. He made garments from an old American flag and screen-printed a prom-like dress to resemble newsprint in order to 'represent the streets of New York, like the posters… pasted onto buildings'.

Part of Adrover's skill was his ability to design for the sartorial differences – both real and reputed – in New York's neighbourhoods: the polished, dressed-up poise of 'uptown' and the grit and recycled aesthetic of 'downtown'. 'Midtown', Adrover's second collection (Autumn/Winter 2000–1), addressed both uptown and downtown clothes. For Midtown Adrover complemented the surprising silhouettes of his asymmetrical skirts and tops with the unexpected lavishness of vintage textiles. Midtown featured a subdued colour palette of browns, blues, grey and occasionally red, along with vintage floral prints. Incongruity reigned: exquisite knitwear; skirts and tops with frayed, disintegrating edges; and baseball caps serving as shoulder pads. Even beyond recycled garments, Midtown used other artefacts or finds – parts of Quentin Crisp's discarded mattress, retrieved from a street corner after the writer's death, are a prime example (opposite). Adrover's deconstructed Burberry coat-turned-dress, also from the Midtown collection, was much discussed (see p.072). One review referred to the dress as 'mocking big labels',[11] and indeed Adrover's take on one of the industry's most prominent luxury products did poke fun at fashion's preoccupation with branding and status. Turned inside out and worn back-to-front, the coat's landmark Burberry plaid enveloped the wearer, while the label loomed prominently on the garment's front. Fashion historian Caroline Evans wrote of Adrover's work, 'Adrover dredged his own cellar for comparable abject pickings and converted them into darkly elegant high-fashion items on the catwalk. Like a rags-to-riches fable of the American Way, Adrover's

Miguel Adrover, dress made from Quentin Crisp's mattress ticking. Autumn/Winter 2000–1. Photo: catwalking.com.

New York scraps were recuperated by the very industry that might be expected to reject such abject leavings.'[12]

Many late-twentieth-century fashion designers have refashioned existing garments or incorporated them into something new, from the late Milanese Moschino (1950–94) to London's Robert Carey-Williams (b. 1965). Yet similar investigations have largely been absent from New York's catwalks. Adrover's politically motivated collections associated a New York-based designer with an avant-garde tradition that, in twentieth-century fashion terms, has largely been European. Adrover explained his motivation:

I cannot do a collection based on trends and flowers when in the city there are bombs.

However, although Adrover's designs provided social commentary and challenged convention, they never strayed too far from it, and so remained aesthetically appealing to a mainstream audience of fashion critics, retail buyers and the fashion press. In 2000, the same year as Midtown, the trade association CFDA awarded Adrover with the annual Perry Ellis Award for best new designer. The fashion journalist Suzy Menkes wrote about Adrover's subversive but likeable clothes: 'The different sensibility of European and American designers (complexity versus commerce) was expressed in a strong show by the Majorcan-born Miguel Adrover… "Midtown" was the show's title, and that expressed perfectly the modern mix of upscale elegance in the fine tailoring and polished makeup with the downtown rawness and recycling. Let's call the new look Uptown With an Edge.'[13]

Adrover, with the financial backing of Pegasus (later the Leiber Group), built a business with international commercial ties. He produced embroideries in far-flung locales such as Egypt and Santo Domingo. For suits he consulted with eminent Brooklyn-based tailor Martin Greenfield as well as with Sicilian tailors in Naples and Catania. Adrover also sourced fabric worldwide: silk from Hong Kong, cotton from Switzerland and wool from Scotland. With Pegasus' financial support, he was able to build the complex network of suppliers and manufacturers he relied on to make high-end clothes of fine quality.

Adrover's overtly political references continued with his Spring/Summer 2001 designs. This collection alluded to a romanticized notion of American history, featuring gingham prairie dresses and Western-wear. More striking were the overt references to political history – in this case the Vietnam War. He alluded to the military uniforms worn in the war through army green or navy-coloured trousers, shirts and jackets, some accented with military badges. Adrover also included patchwork, waistcoats printed with war slogans and a dress made from a much-used army-green trousers and shirt; the dress, torn and dirty, seemed itself to have come from the battlefield (opposite). To sharpen the commentary, Adrover added to the catwalk of polished, professional models a mixture of 'non-models' whose age, body shape or ethnicity boldly defied the norm.

After what were rumoured to be slow sales and an ill-timed Middle Eastern-inspired collection conceived before the September 11 attacks, at the end of 2001 Adrover's backers pulled out. Adrover continued, but he struggled. The *New York Times* reported that 'By spring of this year, his austere clothes languished on sales racks. His Fall 2001 collection, with its Middle Eastern influences, reached stores at a time when Americans were unlikely to embrace such references. By October, Pegasus, which is now known as the Leiber Group, shut down Mr. Adrover's business.'[14] From 2002 until 2005 the designer's annual catwalk presentations (combining two seasons into one show) chronicled his determination. These shows culminated in the presentation of Spring/Summer 2005, Adrover's last collection. Held outside in a Lower East Side park, the clothes revisited the theme of the American West. Less overtly political, but still unorthodox, Adrover's show referenced Native American culture both in the garments (Western leathers, Indian embroidery and handprints) and in the choice of an ethnically mixed model line-up. If his Spring/Summer 2005 designs were more poetic vision than political treatise, perhaps pragmatism was at work. After viewing the show, Suzy Menkes commented: 'Adrover is a genuine creative spirit who established a fashion identity from the start, creating a tailoring of chic severity and finding nobility in ethnicity… But will Adrover get financial support?'[15] Adrover defiantly took his end-of-show bow wearing a T-shirt emblazoned with the words, 'Anyone Seen a Backer?'. This bow was Adrover's last on New York's catwalks. Summing up his experience, he commented that although:

New York is a place where you can find yourself. [It is also] a city which closes the doors on creativity.

The decisions of Miguel Adrover and Tess Giberson to close down their labels invites a critical question. Why is New York – a city with strong traditions of supporting the new and the experimental in fine art, architecture, and the performing arts – inhospitable to avant-garde fashion? Perhaps it is because the avant-garde reputations of other fashion cities eclipse the efforts of New York's few radical fashion labels. That the city's fashion colleges are industry-focused rather than situated within a fine arts curriculum such as London's Central Saint Martins may also be a factor. Whatever the cause, all four avant-gardists expressed a yearning for a more consistently receptive audience, unfavourably comparing the attitude of their host city with the open-mindedness of Paris. That New York's mainstream fashion press alternates between happy surprise in 'discovering' their work and subsequent indifference, even to the extent of ignoring their creations, adds to their concern. As a result, these designers have all reacted either by modifying their designs or their business approach. Perhaps most telling is that two of the four have discontinued their labels altogether.

ABOVE Stella Tennant wearing a Miguel
Adrover design. Spring/Summer 2001.
Photo: Arthur Elgort/*Vogue* © 2001/
2004 Condé Nast Publications Inc.

RIGHT Miguel Adrover, dress made from
a distressed uniform. Spring/Summer
2001. Photo: courtesy of Miguel Adrover.

MENS
WEAR

Duckie Brown, underpants with
attached gloves. Autumn/Winter
2002–3. Photo: PLATON.

MENSWEAR
NEW VOICES, NEW VISIONS

As the clothes examined thus far suggest, the infrastructure of New York's fashion industry has historically been and continues to be focused on women. Most of the high-end clothing and accessories designed and sold there are for women, despite the city's reputation for classic tailoring and the acknowledged skills of its remaining menswear manufacturers. Consequently, the city's press, advertising and retail segments likewise concentrate primarily on womenswear. While this is true for all of the world's major fashion centres, some cities where womenswear dominates have successfully generated influential menswear traditions. London, for example, boasting the centuries-old bespoke craftsmanship of Savile Row's tailors, further claims the 1960s Carnaby Street-fomented transformation in men's fashion. Milan's post-War emergence as Italy's fashion capital not only solidified the country's strong reputation for tailoring but also produced the important late-twentieth-century designers of leading menswear, Giorgio Armani and Gianni Versace. Emphasizing its enthusiasm for men's fashion, Milan hosts separate menswear fashion weeks twice yearly – in contrast to New York, which squeezes men's fashion into its spring and autumn show schedules.

Late twentieth-century New York designers continued this historic indifference by focusing on women's clothes, with menswear as something of an afterthought. In recent years, however, a handful of upscale New York-based designers have defied precedent and prejudice by launching fashion labels exclusively for men. Four in particular provide the discerning male shopper with distinct interpretations of the contemporary male wardrobe: John Varvatos updates traditional sportswear; Duckie Brown infuses classic suiting with whimsy; Alexandre Plokhov references military dress; and Thom Browne champions the urbanity of retro tailoring. These four designers have several things in common. They worked with other designers first, absorbing both technical skills and business acumen. They were in their mid-30s to early 40s when they started out on their own. They have all won industry awards. Most significant to a discussion of contemporary New York fashion is that these four designers represent a broad range of sartorial choices in their differing interpretations of masculinity.

John Varvatos, tailoring from
Autumn/Winter 2005–6. Photo:
Maria Valentino.

JOHN VARVATOS

Of the four designers featured here, menswear specialist John Varvatos was the most experienced by the time he launched his eponymous sportswear and tailoring label. Varvatos (b. 1955), a Michigan native, studied fashion at FIT, then worked for 15 years at Calvin Klein and Ralph Lauren (where he was Vice President of menswear from 1995) until he began his own business in 1999. Looking back on his entrepreneurial timing, he reflected: 'At that moment the market was open to a different point of view. Not a look that was sleek or slick but something more masculine. Ralph Lauren told me, "If you feel that you've got something new to say that is different for the market" then I'd know it was the right moment.'[1]

John Varvato's line is part-owned by VF Corporation, an apparel conglomerate that specializes in denim and sportswear.[2] Their backing enabled Varvatos to open his first independent retail store in 2000 in Manhattan's SoHo, a rare accomplishment for an emerging label. By 2005 there were five John Varvatos stores across America, and over 130 retailers in North America, Europe and Asia carried his clothes. Varvatos also developed his own men's fragrance and skincare line as well as footwear and eyewear. He said:

You can be a specialized niche brand without financial backing. But if you want to be a strong brand with significant space in better department stores you need financial backing. I wouldn't have been able to do what I've done without that.

The Varvatos stores, national retail distribution and a growing list of product categories are all significant brand-building milestones. They indicate that although Varvatos designs for men, he is using the business techniques of late twentieth-century womenswear empires to build a mega-brand.

In addition to secure financial backing, Varvatos' menswear industry experience significantly influenced the pace and scope of his increasing importance. Also facilitating Varvatos' rapid expansion was enthusiastic support from the fashion industry. In June 2000, the Council of Fashion Designers of America (CFDA) awarded Varvatos the annual Perry Ellis Award for Menswear. A year later Varvatos won the CFDA Menswear Designer of the Year Award, which he received again in 2005. His designs receive frequent attention in the mainstream men's fashion press, including publications such as *GQ*, *Details* and *Esquire*.

John Varvatos' decision to design only menswear was carefully calculated – he has revealed that he wanted to focus on, and be the best at, something.[3] Now, he says, '…we're the largest men's designer brand in the stores that we're in'. He attributes his company's rapid growth and industry recognition to three factors. First, his age (he was in his early 40s at the outset) and experience; next, a seasoned production team, whose expertise in overseeing manufacturing 'allows us to execute and deliver'; and finally, VF Corporation's financial backing.

Although Varvatos designs tailored suits, jackets and trousers, he has built his fashion label on sportswear classics – clothes for customers who are 'mixing dressy with casual, resulting in an eclectic look'. Each Varvatos garment co-ordinates with many different outfits. He executes his collections using relaxed construction and a quiet colour palette of beige, browns and greys to create informal, understated ensembles. A typical example (Spring/Summer 2001) features khaki trousers, green

John Varvatos, beige cotton trousers with leather jacket, Spring/Summer 2001. Photo: Maria Valentino.

BELOW LEFT John Varvatos, distressed leather jacket, Autumn/Winter 2006–7. Photo: Maria Valentino.

BELOW BOTTOM John Varvatos, poncho with narrow trousers, Autumn/Winter 2006–7. Photo: Maria Valentino.

BELOW RIGHT John Varvatos, advertising campaign featuring Chris Cornell, Autumn/Winter 2006–7. Photo: Danny Clinch.

cotton T-shirt, mustard-yellow leather jacket and coordinating belt and open-toed sandals (opposite).

Varvatos offers American men updated versions of their wardrobe staples. In his Autumn/Winter 2006–7 collection he included a multitude of leather jacket styles, a reminder of the garment's continuing appeal. The same collection also included further favourites: military boots, distressed denim and khaki trousers. Its advertising campaign used the rugged appeal of singer/songwriter star Chris Cornell, formerly of the rock band Soundgarden, to emphasize Varvatos' traditional masculine styling (below). However, the collection also showed a softer side, featuring more feminine elements such as leather shoulder bags, ponchos and shawls (bottom). With its tough-guy ideal mollified by the occasional accessory, Varvatos' Autumn/Winter 2006–7 collection demonstrated his ability to attire an upscale American everyman.

LIVERPOOL JOHN MOORES UNIVERSITY
Aldham Robarts L.R.C.
TEL 0151 231 3701/3634

DUCKIE BROWN

ABOVE Duckie Brown, plaid suit with
beading, Autumn/Winter 2005–6.
Photo: courtesy of Duckie Brown.

OPPOSITE ABOVE Duckie Brown,
kilt cummerbund and trousers,
Autumn/Winter 2004–5.
Photo: courtesy of PLATON.

OPPOSITE BELOW Duckie Brown,
trompe l'oeil shirt design with jacket
and trousers, Spring/Summer 2006.
Photo: courtesy of PLATON.

While John Varvatos' sportswear-based designs have broad appeal, Steven Cox and Daniel Silver's juxtaposition of whimsy and classic tailoring suggests a more inclusive conception of modern masculinity. The duo founded their menswear label Duckie Brown in 2001. While the designers oppose the characterization of Duckie Brown as a 'gay' label, they want their irreverent ornament and amusing accessories to challenge New York's traditionally staid menswear.

Their professional backgrounds differ. Steven Cox (b. 1967), the lead designer, is British and attended design school in Liverpool. He then spent more than 15 years in New York designing for other firms, including Tommy Hilfiger and Ralph Lauren. Daniel Silver (b. 1958), who is from Toronto, Canada, entered the industry as a glove designer in the 1980s and then spent a dozen years as a television producer. Silver contributes to the designs and also serves as Duckie Brown's business manager.

Duckie Brown presented their early work at Gen Art's annual Fresh Faces in Fashion show during New York Fashion Week in 2003. Publications such as the *New York Times*, the *Wall Street Journal* and *Vogue*'s Style.com covered the event. Another important moment came that same year when the exclusive, influential New York store Barneys invited Duckie Brown to sell their line on its coveted, so-called 'designer floor' on the third level. Steven Cox clarified the significance of being a New York designer in Barneys: 'We found that it's almost like being the local football team, that we're a New York label. The third floor of Barneys is incredible to be on; and because we are the only home team playing there, the sales staff are very much behind us.'[4] Four years after launching, they described their business as 'still very small', quantifying their annual sales as roughly $500,000 per year. However, over two dozen stores around the United States carry their clothes, and well over double that in Japan.

Duckie Brown's designs subvert tradition with caprice. While ensuring that their clothes are essentially wearable, they offer the more adventurous shopper a sartorial alternative beyond the narrow parameters of male fashionability embodied in most American menswear. Silver said:

No matter what we design there is a sensibility that it's totally wearable. Now, it might not be everyone's aesthetic, especially with men, because the roles are so tightly drawn and the lines of what is acceptable and what is not acceptable are so crazy. The essence of Duckie Brown is challenging those things.

Suits – tailored jackets and trousers – are the foundation of Duckie Brown's style. The designers use traditional wool suiting fabric for some tailored garments; others with similarly conservative silhouettes may come in unexpected colours or have unusual embellishment, such as beading or appliqué. One example is Duckie Brown's red and black tartan suit from their Autumn/Winter 2005–6 collection (above). The designers used a traditional Scottish tartan, manufactured by the venerable textile firm Lochcarron, to make a suit of conventional cut and construction. However, they accented the jacket hem with a thick band of tiny

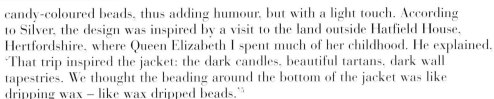

candy-coloured beads, thus adding humour, but with a light touch. According to Silver, the design was inspired by a visit to the land outside Hatfield House, Hertfordshire, where Queen Elizabeth I spent much of her childhood. He explained, 'That trip inspired the jacket: the dark candles, beautiful tartans, dark wall tapestries. We thought the beading around the bottom of the jacket was like dripping wax – like wax dripped beads.'[5]

Fanciful accessories further enliven Duckie Brown's offerings and include a short, jaunty version of a Scottish kilt from the Autumn/Winter 2004–5 collection (below). Of this garment, designed to be worn over trousers, Cox said, 'It's a traditional man's kilt, made in Scotland. Everything is exactly the same as a man's kilt but it's intended to be not a skirt but a cummerbund. It's high-waisted, which is where you placed it, traditionally.' Another whimsical Duckie Brown accessory, first shown in Autumn/Winter 2002–3, is a pair of underpants with gloves attached, which the designers continue to offer each season (see p.091).

Cox and Silver produce most of their garments locally at factories in New Jersey, Queens and Brooklyn. Silver explained the decision to manufacture locally: 'The only way that we can really maintain control of the collection is if we have access to the factories. That's one reason why we have everything made here. It would be cheaper for us in Europe and in Asia but we don't have the relationships with those factories like we do here. So, there would be much more of a chance of our order being pushed back because they'd received a million dollar order from Ralph or Calvin. For us to remain financially solvent, deliver on time and maintain quality, it became apparent very quickly that we really had to make as much as we could out of the New York area.'

Cox and Silver also praised the flexibility and helpfulness of local factories willing to produce small orders of just a few styles. 'People, especially in the New York area, have been extremely helpful and supportive. The factories have been behind us. They've been willing to make up 12 of one jacket or just two dozen of one pair of trousers.'

With no financial backers or investors to satisfy, Cox and Silver design to please themselves. Cox, who spent years designing according to someone else's aesthetic, revels in this creative liberty. He said, 'It's important that we laugh because I didn't laugh at a lot of places I worked. We can do what we want. There are no people telling us what to do and we have fun. We are not saving anybody's life. It is only clothes and we want to have fun doing it. It's been the best four years I've ever had.'

ALEXANDRE PLOKHOV, CLOAK

Alexandre Plokhov's hard-edged designs for his menswear-only label Cloak present a marked contrast to Duckie Brown's whimsy. Originally from Narofominsk, Russia (50 miles south-east of Moscow), Plokhov (b. 1967) has run this New York label since 1999. After studying at Chicago's International Academy of Merchandising and Design, he then ran a custom tailoring business there for several years. He moved to New York in 1998 where he initially worked for Marc Jacobs as a men's pattern-maker.

The motivation for Plokhov's focus on menswear was a desire to perfect the man's suit. 'For a long time I was trying to figure out what I wanted to do. For the life of me I couldn't figure out how to make a suit; it was a kind of a challenge, like waving a red flag. Eventually, I progressed and figured it out.'[6] The constancy of menswear appealed to Plokhov. He sees 'less of a disposable factor to men's clothing', clarifying that 'the seasons matter, but it's not so frivolous'. Comparing men's fashion to women's, Plokhov said, 'It's a bit more serious and it's not so psychotic. With womenswear one day it's Russian, the next day it's bohemian hippy, the third day it's Romeo Gigli. Menswear isn't quite like this.' Further, Plokhov likes the relative calmness of menswear, considering it less celebrity- and media-driven than womenswear: 'In all fairness, it doesn't go in any magazines. Men don't shop from magazines. Most of them find a designer that fits them and reflects their personality and just keep buying. Yes, it does help if a band wears your clothes and the photo appears in the media or in a magazine spread but that is secondary to the design, the fit and on-time delivery. It's not driven by a profile in *Vogue*.'

Plokhov's adopted city influences his designs: his clothes make more use of visual references to the metropolis than do those of his contemporaries. Plokhov maintains that his colours and aesthetic reflect New York's urban atmosphere. He explained, 'If you look at [my] colour palette it is fairly dark and luxuriating. Cloak aesthetics are influenced by New York's cool skirt of warmth and loneliness and its slight danger too. When I was in Russia, that's how all of us perceived New York.' He added, 'It's the only place I wanted to be.'

Like Duckie Browne, Alexandre Plokhov works mainly with New York-area factories, and his experience of searching out those that meet his particular needs mirrors the efforts of his peers. Although navigating these difficulties was challenging for Plokhov, he praised the quality of local production: 'There are factories that can do any kind of level of work, which is comparable to anything the Europeans can do, from hand-tailoring to beautiful shirt-making. The only thing that is missing in New York is knitwear. But we have beautiful leather factories and a beautiful hand-tailoring factory that we work with in Brooklyn. So, everything could be found. The problem is the variety of these sources is quite limited. It's not like in Italy where there's a region that has 20 factories that just make shirts. That does not apply here. There is one factory that makes shirts. But now we know them.'

During his first years of business, Plokhov said, he saw few signs of support from the city's established fashion industry. But in 2004, after submitting an application to the first CFDA/*Vogue* Fashion Fund he was singled out as one of ten finalists, and then – along with the sportswear line Habitual – selected as a runner-up (see p.101). At that point, according to Plokhov, 'all of a sudden everything changed'. The Fund awarded Plokhov $50,000 to build his business. In addition, it assigned him an industry mentor, Julie Gilhart, Senior Vice President and Fashion Director of Barneys. Plokhov described the impact of this mentorship: 'All of a sudden I could get advice [about] trademark protection or where to make this or make that. You know who to call, and these people *answer* the phone call, as opposed to it goes to the secretary and never goes anywhere. I'm a grown-up person. I don't need somebody telling me that pink is going to be big next season. But sometimes I need advice when I'm about to make a strategic decision. Having the ear of people like Julie Gilhart from Barneys, it helps.[ ]

What distinguished Plokhov from the other Fashion Fund finalists were his sombre designs that romanticized a tough, flinty masculine ideal. Referencing distinctive images of masculinity, Plokhov's garments have been inspired by a range of male costumes, including the military man, arctic explorer and safari hunter. Plokhov's safari jacket from Spring/Summer 2006 suggests how the designer appropriates elements of earlier men's fashions. The outfit was clearly designed for urban living rather than for hunting exotic animals: the designer used the white cotton canvas, generous pockets and belted waist of the original, but adopted a contemporary slim silhouette and paired the jacket with dressy charcoal-grey evening trousers.

Throughout Cloak's collections a number of designs have referred to military garments and accessories. Plokhov attributes his interest in uniforms to a curiosity about their history and their construction. He explained:

With uniforms, I want to study them and discover something new for myself. For Spring 2005 I did this braid, this epaulet – it's like a braid with brass tips. That [once] had a meaning! The number of knots, the type of knot that was used, it was actually a language. And to me, yes, it looks really cool, dangling things, but there was a meaning behind it, there was a reason.[7]

The epaulette Plokhov described adorned a black cotton coat from Spring/Summer 2005 (see p.100). Inspiration for the coat came from a priest's cassock; the garment featured slim arms and a trim, elongated silhouette. The coat's precise construction is proof of Plokhov's successful struggle to master the exacting techniques of traditional tailoring, while its dark colouring and idiosyncratic combination of military and religious references epitomize Cloak's severe style.

OPPOSITE TOP Cloak, updated safari
jacket with trousers, Spring/Summer
2006. Photo: courtesy of Cloak.

OPPOSITE BOTTOM Cloak, black
cassock with black cord aiguillette,
Spring/Summer 2005. Photo:
courtesy of Cloak.

ABOVE Alexandre Plokhov, Cloak,
2004. Models with Plokhov as
a finalist in the CFDA/*Vogue*
Fashion Fund competition. Photo:
Arthur Elgort/*Vogue* © 2001/2004
Condé Nast Publications Inc.

THOM BROWNE

Thom Browne, the bands My Best Friend and Soft performing at Bergdorf Goodman Man wearing Thom Browne designs, 2005. Photo: Jacob Brown. Originally published on *Paper* magazine's website.

Also preoccupied with the details of cut and construction is custom tailor Thom Browne (b. 1965). Browne looks back to the sensibility of the 1950s and early 1960s for his masculine sartorial model, reinterpreting a classic suit as the ideal expression of modern masculinity. With narrow trouser legs, short jackets and trouser hems grazing the shoe top, the silhouette of a Thom Browne suit is particular and specific; the look is what the designer insists his clients adopt. Although Browne designs a ready-to-wear line in addition to his bespoke designs and does make garments other than suits, he wants to encourage a younger generation to adopt the suit as a kind of all-occasion uniform.

Browne started his label in 2001. This was after several years of acting in Los Angeles and then a move to New York where he worked first for Armani and then became head of menswear design at the retail chain Club Monaco. In the late 1990s Browne made his first suits for himself with the help of a tailor. Browne said:

When I started to do my thing I made five suits… [according to] exactly the [style] that I was always looking for, for myself. That's all I did. Whether or not people were going to like it was not the point. I just knew that this is what I wanted and I thought, well, if I wanted it then there must be somebody else that wants it.[8]

Browne took a year to get his first jacket right. He said, 'I worked hard with my tailor. Take the shoulders in and then take the armhole up, and if you change one thing you can totally throw off the balance of a jacket. I think it took me about 19 jackets until I got what I wanted.'[9]

Browne described these early years as very hard. Based out of his New York apartment, a complete unknown, he said, 'At first… it was just friends doing me a favour by buying a suit.' Those first clients questioned the fit of Browne's designs, suggesting that the jackets were too short or the trousers too tight. Eventually, Browne said, he would convince them. Financial difficulties were even more challenging because he started without a backer. He explained:

Financially it was tough because I wanted to do it all on my own and that's one of the reasons why I started doing it all custom because I didn't have to pay for anything myself upfront. It was kind of the chicken way of doing it but I didn't want to overwhelm myself with the burden of overheads. I wanted all my interest to go into the actual clothing.

Browne's earliest marketing strategy was literally self-centred and maximally low-cost: he wore his own designs when he went out, and people started asking where they could buy them. This strategy served well enough to allow him, in 2002, to open a studio on Little West 12th Street in New York's Meatpacking District, where his company's custom work is still done. As Browne's reputation grew, some influential retailers – New York's Bergdorf Goodman Men and Jeffrey's as well as Fred Segal (Los Angeles) and Colette (Paris) – began carrying his ready-to-wear line. Much wider industry recognition and support came in the 2005 CFDA/*Vogue* Fashion Fund competition: Thom Browne was named one of ten finalists. A *Vogue* photograph intended to illustrate the special characteristics of his clothing shows that Browne (centre front) is his own best model (see p.104–105). 'Browne's purpose is to get young men back into suits,' read *Vogue's* editorial copy, 'and he wants his jackets and trousers to look as cool as his purported customers' favorite jeans and T-shirt – and even be worn in lieu of them.'[10]

With a design studio, regular clients and relationships with influential retailers, Browne has achieved much since starting out. Keenly aware of the importance of recognizable uniqueness in his bespoke clothing, Browne defended its high cost: 'The challenge is that people have to realize that it's more expensive. It's hand-made clothing… each piece is actually touched by the designer. It's so much more unique and so much more special. I think stores are lucky to actually have it, not because it's mine but because it elevates the level of what they're putting in their stores.'

However, Browne stressed that his ready-to-wear designs are of the same quality as his custom suits – they are simply 'pre-made'. In September 2005 he staged an event showcasing his ready-to-wear designs at Bergdorf Goodman. Photographs of the proceedings, featuring performances by several bands dressed in Browne suits suggest – even in still images on the page – how his designs look on the body and in motion (left).

Before designing his own line Browne occasionally shopped for himself at vintage clothing stores in search of the right fit and style. However, he avoids literal recreations of the stiff fabrics and heaviness of mid-twentieth-century suiting but rather adapts the sharp, formal sophistication of 1950s tailoring to the casual lifestyles of his urban clients (he claims to run his own fine wool suits through the washing machine to give them a rumpled informality). Expressing his aspiration for how his contemporary interpretation of the classic suit might influence men's fashion Browne said, 'I think so many young guys have gotten away from [tailored] clothing in general because of a fussy, over-the-top feeling. My biggest hope is that young guys get back into this whole [suit] thing.'

In a country where historically the dandy has been somewhat suspect, it is significant that at the turn of the millennium, four talented designers founded fashionable, high-end menswear companies. Directly relevant to their success is that these designers appeared on the scene at a time when many disparate enterprises had been working with particular vigour to convince American men to spend more on personal appearance.[11] While many of their designs are available in only a limited way through upscale, mainly urban retailers, their very existence indicates a changing New York fashion culture.

Thom Browne and models wearing the designer's suits, 2005. Photo: Norman Jean Roy, originally published in *Vogue*.

CELEBRITY

Lost Art by Jordan Betten, leather
trousers worn by Sheryl Crow in
concert, Woodstock 1999. Photo:
Tara Canova.

CELEBRITY
FASHION AND FAME

Christian Joy, Shrimp Dress worn
by Karen O of the Yeah Yeah Yeahs,
Kentish Town Forum, London, June
2003. Photo: Empics.

In contrast to designers who start fashion lines that cater to a market niche such as
menswear, others use the cult of celebrity to establish their fashion labels. Today's
celebrities are always 'on stage', and thus seem familiar. Yet the nature of modern
celebrity is that although we may think we know much about a popular personality,
ultimately they remain inaccessible. The powerful appeal of this dichotomy cuts across
the demographics of age, socio-economic levels and ethnicity. For fashion designers
who manipulate this appeal, the street recognition, paparazzi entourages and
preoccupation with wardrobe contents and grooming habits that accompany modern
celebrity make the famous an ideal vehicle for marketing clothes. President John F.
Kennedy's advisors standardized the process of modern celebrity manufacture. Aided
by his father, wife and a host of accomplished photographers, Kennedy used the press,
photography and television in a way that both helped Americans identify personally
with the Kennedys while at the same time making them seem larger than life.[1] What
was a new process in Kennedy's time is today a predictable course to achieving fame.
According to Pamela Church Gibson, fashion's relationship to celebrity is today completely
disproportionate. 'Young designers are forced from the outset to try and hitch their
fortunes to the celebrity bandwagon if they are to achieve recognition of any kind.'[2]

Using celebrity to promote designer wares is nothing new. The nineteenth-century
couturier Charles Frederick Worth capitalized on the patronage of such clients as the
English actress Lillie Langtry. The early twentieth-century English actress Gertrude
Lawrence publicized Norman Hartnell. Such admired performers popularized chosen
designers by wearing their creations on and off stage. Towards the end of the twentieth
century this practice intensified as fashion designers enlisted famous people to wear
their clothes to high-profile events, thus using the cult of others' celebrity to their own
ends. Popular musicians were particularly important promotional vehicles for late
twentieth-century designers. Of these, the most well-known examples include Vivienne
Westwood and Malcolm McLaren, who shaped the sartorial identity of 1970s British
punk band the Sex Pistols, and French designer Jean Paul Gaultier, who crafted the
sculptural stage costumes for Madonna's 1990 'Blonde Ambition' tour. Wider
subcultural fashion trends connected with specific performers include Duran Duran's
association with the 1980s New Romantic movement or the late Nirvana lead singer
Kurt Cobain's links with early 1990s Grunge style. The New York-based Stephen
Sprouse designed 1970s stage costumes for Debbie Harry of the band Blondie.[3]
Similarly, Betsy Johnson designed for the Velvet Underground and Anna Sui has
outfitted Sheryl Crow and Stevie Nicks.

Like these designers of now oracular status, Christian Joy, Craig Robinson and
Sean 'Diddy' Combs have also used the cult of celebrity, either their own or other
people's, to launch their fashion labels. This edited designer grouping represents
a range of approaches to a business strategy that has long been identified with New
York's fashion culture, one that can be less about designing fashion than about
costuming spectacles. Their target customers differ in age and thus their clothes
range in price. Joy and Combs offer affordably priced street wear (many of their
clothes are priced under $150) for a younger generation. Robinson's sophisticated,
bespoke suits are intended for city dressing and priced for grown-ups: a custom
suit costs around between $2000 and $4000. Although Joy, Robinson and Combs
together constitute only a small representation of a much larger phenomenon, their
methods illustrate how powerful, even essential, the association with celebrity
remains for some New York designers.

CHRISTIAN JOY

Crowd, (including a few Karen O look-alikes), at a 2003 Yeah Yeah Yeahs' concert, Melbourne. Photo: Nicholas Zinner.

At 26, Christiane Joy Hultquist (b. 1973), now Christian Joy, was the youngest of this publication's three designers connected to celebrity to start her own label. The self-taught Joy was born in Marion, Iowa and attended Oberlin College in Ohio. She began designing for the then 21-year-old Karen O (for Orzolek) between 2000 and 2001. Orzolek is the flamboyant lead singer of one of New York's rowdiest bands, the Yeah Yeah Yeahs. The band's music was summarized by *The New Yorker* magazine as a combination of surreal lyrics with a pop 'economy, momentum, personality and pleasure'.[4] Founded in 2000, they were unrecorded until 2002, yet in 2003 their debut album, 'Fever to Tell', went gold. The Yeah Yeah Yeahs' live performances on the international music circuit have spawned both music fans and fashion copycats, with Karen O's rebel wardrobe part of the band's attraction. Said Orzolek:

The Karen O look-a-likes are my favourite. They come to the shows all decked out Karen O style. I feel a lot of love from my girls.[5]

She continued, 'We are influencing a certain style… using really obnoxious colours and wild patterns. All these girls (and boys) copy it but also make it their own. They come to the concerts [wearing] the same colours, patterns and haircuts, but interpreted slightly differently.' Said one 16-year-old British Karen O fan, 'Two friends and I got haircuts like Karen's – the one with the shaggy fringe over the eyes. Part of her appeal, and why we want to be like her, is because she's not like anyone else.'[6]

Karen O wore Joy's designs in some of her earliest performances. At that time, Joy had found her way to fashion by first working in a series of Brooklyn clothing boutiques. Without formal training, in 2000 she began to make clothes simply by deconstructing T-shirts and other garments to sell locally. Soon after, Karen O, a frequent customer at the shop where Christian Joy worked, invited her to see the band perform. Joy offered to lend her something to wear that night – a slashed-up prom dress – and a designer/client relationship began. Joy said that this first design for O complemented the young singer's irreverent, extroverted on-stage persona, a style that includes, in Joy's words, 'Pouring beer on herself on-stage, and on the audience, rolling around on the floor and rolling off the stage.' Joy, on the other hand, remembered her reaction to seeing her clothes on stage for the first time: 'I was shy and awkward.'[7] At the prom dress performance Joy recalled that Karen shouted out to the audience, 'Do you want to know where I got this dress?', and credited Joy. Since then Joy has designed almost all of Karen O's costumes for the band's live performances.

The Yeah Yeah Yeahs started out as a Brooklyn band with a small loyal fan base. A profile in *Rolling Stone* magazine stated in 2002, 'A year ago they were a promising little unsigned trio with fans in at least two of New York City's five boroughs. Today – without even releasing a full-length album – they are a promising little unsigned band with fans around the world.' While band members Brian Chase and Nick Zinner do not don special stage clothes, Karen O now regularly changes costumes during a performance. Neither polished nor polite, the outfits have featured rips, slashes, painting and padding in odd places. Orzolek's Joy-designed stage outfits have included silver padded bodysuits; graffiti-scarred cocktail dresses; and snug-fitting mini-dresses over fishnet stockings, all worn with Converse hightop sneakers, bright red lipstick and Orzolek's signature single glove. The singer likes Joy's experimentation with different materials, citing as an example a green and silver spandex bodysuit with paisley fans attached to the elbows and knees. She said, 'When the light hit me I was completely silver.' However, the non-breatheable material made the outfit bearable for only several songs, since wearing it onstage 'felt like a sauna'. Karen O now regularly changes Joy's costumes during a performance. According to Orzolek:

Christian's imagination far exceeds mine. I give her complete 100% blind faith. I see what she makes for me only on the day of the performance. That takes balls!

For Joy, designing Orzolek's stage clothes involves more than just creating a look or an impression. Crucially, Joy's designs also provide her client with props for performance. A favourite example of Orzolek's is a 2003 design called the Shrimp Dress – a patterned pink day dress accessorized with a stole in the form of a large stuffed shrimp (see p.109). During a climactic part of a live London performance Orzolek spontaneously tore the shrimp to pieces on stage and then, as she put it, 'distributed it to the gods as a sacrifice', to the delight of her fans. A later design also served as a memorable stage prop. Joy described it as a 'Day of the Dead' bodysuit with a skeleton form painted on it (see p.112). She said:

Christian Joy, 'Day of the Dead' bodysuit worn by Karen O of the Yeah Yeah Yeahs, Brixton Academy, London, November 2004. Photo: Empics.

It was one of the only costumes I really had the chance to take to its fullest; usually I'm strapped for time. Around the hood I embroidered long strands of thread in blue, yellow and red that hung down over her face like a voodoo wig. There were red and white strands of threads on the cuffs and wooden beads at the elbows and at the back, strips of shredded, striped fabric. I also made a three-dimensional heart that sat on top of the costume; it had veins that came up to her neck. Finally, it came with 9 feet of stuffed blue spandex intestines that she could pull out and throw into the audience. I loved that costume!

While Joy's silver bodysuits and outré accessories for Orzolek are more costume than fashion, Joy also assembles low-key looks for some of the singer's performances, designs that the singer's teen and twenty-something fans easily copy and adapt. O's wardrobe staples are the mini dresses, T-shirts and mini skirts she wears with fishnet stockings and high-top sneakers. Young fans can even find websites with home fashion-making tips on creating clothes à la Karen O. *Elle Girl*, on its 'DIY Fashion' page, included a Christian Joy recipe for turning an old pair of shoes into 'a thing of punk rock beauty'.

Christian Joy's business, though still small, is growing. The designer has learned how to make patterns, find fabric and handle the steady stream of orders for the Christian Joy line of clothing sold via her own website (at the time of writing she has no other retail outlet, but she has expressed an interest in opening her own store). Joy makes the clothes herself with the help of a seamstress and a few interns at her Greenpoint, Brooklyn studio. Like almost all her fashion contemporaries, she views the life of the aspiring designer as difficult. 'Coming up with the money to make a collection isn't easy. It's hard to keep up with fashion shows, showrooms and press if you don't have a lot of money or someone backing you.' Serving as the sole designer to a cult band's lead singer may leave Joy more vulnerable to entrepreneurial pitfalls than her peers. She declared, 'I wouldn't be where I am today without the band's success.' Like the Yeah Yeah Yeahs' fan base, which has grown from a small group of in-the-know locals to an increasingly mainstream, international following, Joy's designs are now coveted by people outside the club circuit, and conventional press vehicles such as *Time, Elle, W* and the *New York Times* have showcased Joy's work. Expressing little ambivalence about this, Joy said, 'The mainstream magazines are starting to ask about the clothes. If those girls are asking about it and if the general public like it, then great!'

CRAIG ROBINSON

RIGHT Craig Robinson, 'cavalry jacket'
worn by Josh Garza, drummer of
the Secret Machines, Autumn/Winter
2006–7. Photo: Rudy Archuleta.

OPPOSITE Craig Robinson, 'Carter'
3-piece light wool suit worn by
musician Jon Spencer, Autumn/Winter
2006–7. Photo: Rudy Archuleta.

Another designer who has prospered with the success of musician clients is bespoke tailor Craig Robinson (b.1972). Unlike Christian Joy, who designs for one high-profile client, Robinson has dressed a number of New York-area bands. The designer, who at the age of 29 established what he called his 'full fledged fashion label' in 2003, credits his early success in part to his association with bands such as Calla, Secret Machines, Interpol and Dead Combo. Robinson has dressed these musicians and others in his polished, sharply tailored suits. In designing for musicians, Robinson adheres to a long tradition of promoting fashion labels through enlisting performers to wear the clothes on stage. For the bands, wearing Robinson's polished designs gives them a distinct sartorial identity. For Robinson the growing celebrity of his clients makes his label more conspicuous and connects it with the downtown cool of the city's music scene. He reflected on this symbiosis:

Ten years ago, in the mid-1990s, New York didn't have a great rock-and-roll scene – it had fizzled. Then there was a boom. I made pants and shirts and other things for bands that used to be small local kids. Our business grew as they sold more records, and now they're big bands signed up with major record labels.[8]

Robinson understands why his clothes appeal to performers. 'They like my edgy suits. We do a high-end product now and now they can afford it.' Robinson's made-to-measure designs are snug-fitting, constructed from heavy woollen fabrics and often paired with high-collared, brightly coloured striped shirts and wide ties. The suit jackets boast exaggerated lapels and peplum vents or what Robinson calls 'skirted backs'. These details lend his suits a tough-guy air, which has been

amplified in recent collections by accessorizing with a gun holster (which his well-travelled clients use for iPods or mobile phones). Fashion curator Andrew Bolton described Robinson's silhouette: 'It's very tightly tailored, with sharp jacket details. His suits really emphasize and elongate a man's body.'[9]

Consistent with the backgrounds of a number of designers linked to celebrity, Robinson has no formal fashion training. At the age of 23 he moved to New York from New Mexico and started his fashion career by working for a Manhattan milliner. He then spent time at clothing companies in Paris and Milan before returning to New York to attempt to start his own design business and finally establishing his label in 2001. Two years later, in the autumn of 2003, he opened his atelier on lower Fifth Avenue. He enjoys the fact that his address links his business to a neighbourhood historically associated with the city's tailoring trade. However, he confessed that taking out the lease on the premises seemed an extravagant move. 'When I signed the lease I shut my eyes and said, "I'll take it!" Then I walked out and said, "How in the hell am I going to pay for this?" Now I've grown into the price, but in the beginning... I couldn't sleep at night.' Robinson then purchased better equipment, began using higher quality fabric and spent long hours mastering construction techniques.

For the self-taught Robinson, this technical evolution was connected to a mentor. Robinson recalled:

One day a gentleman named Ernesto came into my store. He told me my designs and pieces were good but needed fine-tuning. I listened. He was a master tailor that took me under his wing and helped me learn the techniques I would need to get to the place I wanted.

LIVERPOOL JOHN MOORES UNIVERSITY
Aldham Roberts L.R.C.
TEL. 0151 231 3701/3634

Robinson now works with a team of technically skilled tailors who assist him in creating his made-to-measure designs. After years of careful searching, the designer has gathered together these skilled craftsmen (he calls them his 'old cranky Italian guys') who do much of the sewing under his direction. Like many of the New York designers who produce their clothes locally, Robinson is proud that he is helping to preserve the knowledge and technical skills of what may be the city's last generation of garment-makers. 'We're about keeping the talent and craft here in New York,' he said.

Robinson's conscious combination of musician clients and self-taught craftsmanship resembles that of Jordan Betten (see *Atelier*). While Betten's leather and suede creations exemplify the talent of New York's accomplished artisans, they are equally compelling as examples of celebrity construction, given that a number of musicians wear Betten's designs both on stage and off. What performers may appreciate about Lost Art's bespoke leather and suede garments is that they fit the wearer perfectly. Also, their fringed, beaded details move dramatically on stage. Lost Art's hint of 'the West' in these clothes appeals particularly to country-and-western and rock musicians such as folk-rock star Sheryl Crow, country music superstar Willie Nelson and rock-and-roller Lenny Kravitz.[10] What Betten and Robinson have in common is they have both made use of celebrity customers while simultaneously building reputations through the quality of their craft.

The progression of Robinson's designs towards crisp, more precise tailoring is linked both to his mastering of construction techniques and to an evolving dress code for his musician clients. According to one journalist, 'Ever since retro garage rock bands… showed up on MTV a couple of years ago in skinny ties, blazers and shaggy hair, the push to dress more like rock stars and less like record geeks – baggy jeans and T-shirts – has been gaining momentum.'[11] In Robinson's view, as the young bands aged, their clothing requirements changed. The one-time uniform of jeans and T-shirts gave way to a more polished dress code for many musicians and sometimes their fans, who were now edging out of their 20s and into their 30s. According to Robinson the bands in New York 'have gotten smarter, more polite. They don't spit on people in the front row anymore. Everyone is really into the music, into the art of it. Now it's cool to be successful and wear a suit on stage. Today it's cool to be downtown and dressed up and I've played a part in that gentrification.'

The singer and musician Ezra Reich, a New York native, formed his electronic pop band in 2003 and has performed at a number of New York's Lower East Side music venues including Tonic, Pianos and Sin-é. Reich claims to have worn Robinson's designs at nearly all of his performances. He explained Robinson's appeal: 'Both my look and my music are very 1980s electro-pop and so are very visual and very colourful. Craig's designs represent elegant, well-crafted tailoring. The success of Craig's look is based on the fact that there are few people on the scene who are doing what he's doing.'[12] Reich confirmed the notion of the mutually beneficial designer/musician relationship by adding, 'A number of the bands he designs for wear a lot of black. With me, Craig gets to push the envelope and do a lot more colour. He takes pleasure in creating clothes like that.' Reich cited a design Robinson crafted for his 2005 United Kingdom tour, which was 'an electric-blue jumpsuit; part NASA, the Clash and Elvis'. Reich models similarly bold ensembles on Robinson's website, which includes a photograph of Reich in a close-fitting, wide-lapelled, red suit with a high-collared, black shirt and geometric print tie (see p.115). The portrait, styled with a retro-1980s touch, illustrates both a musician's adoption of Robinson as a designer and the way in which Robinson would like his clothes to be worn. Robinson is clearly proud of the patronage of his musician clients and relishes using celebrity in this way to further his design success. He said, 'We haven't got a movie yet but we'll try.'

Craig Robinson, suit, shirt and tie worn by Ezra Reich. Photo: Rudy Archuleta.

LIVERPOOL JOHN MOORES UNIVERSITY
LEARNING & INFORMATION SERVICES

SEAN 'DIDDY' COMBS
FOR SEAN JOHN

While Christian Joy and Craig Robinson employ the time-honoured practice of using the celebrity of others to promote their clothes, a more recent phenomenon is the celebrity musician-turned-designer. In 2004, fashion journalist Suzy Menkes had observed, 'It seems that anyone in America can produce a collection – as long as they are already famous.'[13] While sports heroes from Renée Lacoste in the 1930s to Tiger Woods in the 2000s and, more recently, famous models[14] have started their own clothing lines, from the late 1990s a number of musicians began to use the cult of their own celebrity to launch careers as fashion designers. A range of incentives may inspire such ventures, including vanity, money, image promotion and creative fulfilment. Whatever the motivation, the turn of the twenty-first century saw a number of performers attempt to make the transition from fame to fashion. What makes a celebrity a successful designer? In part it is creating clothes that are an extension of their own personal brand, or public persona. However, the clothes and the way that they are presented must also offer something more. For while people want to belong, they also want to avoid being seen as a slavish follower.

One of the most high-profile celebrity-turned-designers is Sean 'Diddy' Combs. The rap singer and hip-hop producer founded his Sean John label in 1998, setting a precedent for what soon became a steady stream of fame-to-fashion ventures. While other rap or hip-hop stars have used their celebrity to help establish vanity brands, what is significant about Combs is that he has done so within the confines of the mainstream fashion industry, and in half a decade built his clothing line into a formidable business.

Hip-hop's global dress code is experiencing a reprise and its look has evolved. As fashion historians Robin Chandler and Nuri Chandler-Smith have observed, 'While old-school hip-hop may have been nurtured within poverty, recent hip-hop promotes high-end acquisition', such as expensive sneakers and jewellery.[15] Hip-hop's newer leanings towards luxury make it easier for a designer like Combs to add in more high-end, expensive clothes such as suits and furs (and later a dressy womenswear line) to a fashion label founded on streetwear staples such as jeans, baseball caps and athletic tops. For Combs, this formula has been a financial success. Its combination of high end and affordable, dressed-up and denim illustrates, as the academic Van Dyk Lewis has written, that hip-hop music and its sartorial expression has a double identity as 'both the voice of alienated, frustrated youth and a multi-billion dollar cultural industry'.[16] In the past decade people of different ethnicities and economic backgrounds began aspiring to be the 'other'. Thus inner-city youth has co-opted establishment brands such as 'preppy' Ralph Lauren and deluxe Gucci (and Tommy Hilfiger long before) while white middle-class kids have championed hip-hop gear.

As a driving-force bringing hip-hop music into the mainstream, Combs has both led and benefited from this cultural crossover. He has used the influence of his record label Bad Boy Entertainment, founded in 1993, along with a savvy cultivation of his own public image, to craft himself as the public face of rap. Thus the musician and music producer was well positioned to join those profitably popularizing hip-hop's street wear and sports styles. In this venture, Combs followed the established success of Russell Simmons, hip-hop's elder statesman whose Phat Farm clothing line, founded in 1994, promotes urban, hip-hop-inspired garments.[17]

Combs intends the Sean John sportswear collection to be 'sophisticated fashion forward clothing that also reflected an urban sensibility'.[18] While he aggressively

OPPOSITE LEFT Sean 'Diddy' Combs for Sean John, jumpsuit and fur-trimmed coat. Autumn/Winter 2003–4. Photo: courtesy of Sean 'Diddy' Combs for Sean John.

OPPOSITE RIGHT Sean 'Diddy' Combs for Sean John, parka, top and trousers. Autumn/Winter 2003–4. Photo: courtesy of Sean 'Diddy' Combs for Sean John.

ABOVE Sean John store, opened on 5th Avenue, New York, 2004.

Gwen Stefani for L.A.M.B., models
wearing Spring/Summer 2005
collection. Photo: courtesy of L.A.M.B.

markets his fashion label via the cult of his own persona (both his website and Fifth
Avenue store play his music continuously) he has consciously crafted his fashion
label according to a conventional fashion-industry formula. The Sean John offices
are on Broadway in mid-town Manhattan. Combs (like Simmons' womenswear line
Baby Phat) has presented his collection on the catwalk of New York Fashion Week.
In Sean John's first year, the Council of Fashion Designers of America (CFDA)
nominated Combs for its Perry Ellis Award for Menswear. In 2004 he received the
CFDA's Designer of the Year award. Combs' Sean John label is available at his
flagship Sean John store opposite the New York Public Library on Fifth Avenue
as well as at mainstream American department stores such as Bloomingdale's and
Macy's. The *International Herald Tribune* recently announced, 'The leader of
the celebrity pack is Sean "P. Diddy" Combs, who has parlayed his own personal
swagger into a menswear business that is a genuine success.'[19] Thus, through
association with music and his own celebrity, Combs has supplemented his
entertainment credentials to become the head of a powerful taste-making empire
that generates around $400 million annually and employs roughly 600 people.[20]

Fashion brands such as Sean John have become increasingly canny in
transforming the cult of celebrity into saleable wares. While the music may start
out as the product, eventually the celebrities themselves become the item for
consumption. The Los Angeles-based lead singer Gwen Stefani founded her clothing
line L.A.M.B. after the launch of her first solo album 'Love, Angel, Music, Baby'
in 2004. In her choice of timing, Stefani became one of a number of performer-
turned-designers who were counting on a built-in fan base for ready-made
customers.[21] The singer insists that she designs the line specifically to suit her own
taste, saying, 'The clothes are inspired by my music and cycle of recording. They
are purely selfish, aimed at my own fantasy, at things I would want to wear. I don't
think about inspiring anyone else.'[22] Such deliberate personal references encourage
admirers of Stefani's own eclectic ensembles to buy the L.A.M.B. line in order to
replicate the pop star's style. L.A.M.B.'s cultural hybrid mix met with comparatively
warm critical appraisal, with buyers from both upscale American retailers (L.A.M.B.
clothing is available at Saks Fifth Avenue and Barneys, for example) as well as
influential international boutiques (Colette in Paris and London's Harvey Nichols)
electing to carry the L.A.M.B. line.

While it may seem a truism that 'celebrity sells' the strategy of using one's
own fame to launch a fashion line can backfire, since there will always be shoppers
who remain resolutely hostile to the whole idea ('I'm too smart to fall for that').
Robert Burke, the former fashion director of Bergdorf Goodman, dismissed celebrity
designers in general by saying, 'I find some of it insulting. It is a little arrogant to
say, "I am a designer."'[23] In recent years, Bloomingdale's, which carries both the
Sean Jean line and L.A.M.B., chose not to take on Jennifer Lopez's 'Sweetface' label.
Barneys, too, declined. Perhaps what troubles such fashion traditionalists is that
celebrity designers often lack technical training and industry know-how, thus
forcing them to hand over crucial tasks, indeed sometimes the actual design vision,
to someone else. Such delegation can result in clothes designed by others and simply
marketed by the star. Said fashion director Julie Gilhart, 'The customer is too savvy
at our store. You can have a lot of vibe, but it has got to be a good product.'[24]

EPILOGUE

....

The careers of many emerging New York designers are linked to the city's creative dynamism. New York inspires, nurtures and helps sustain entrepreneurial fashion design. However, there may be cause for future concern. The continually rising costs associated with living and working in Manhattan, and the logistical difficulties of being located in New York's cheaper boroughs, may make the city simply unaffordable and impractical for designers now waiting in the wings. A 2005 study by the Center for an Urban Future, a New York research group that analyses urban policy issues, indicates that the steady increase in New York rents has started to drive artists and makers to other cities.[1] Potential repercussions of a diminished creative class could weaken New York's fashion culture.

New York now faces fashion competition from other American cities, notably Los Angeles, which is actively promoting its own designers and a fashion week schedule separate from New York's. European and Asian cities such as Berlin and Shanghai are likewise positioning themselves as attractive potential bases for young designers. In spite of such challenges, at the moment New York retains its allure and remains vital as a world fashion city. The number and variety of this book's start-up stories show that around the turn of the millennium, during political and economic, even terrorist crises, New York's myriad mechanisms supporting young design talent have stayed firmly in place.

NOTES

PREFACE
1   Interview with the author, 25 July 2005

NEW YORK FASHION IN CONTEXT
1   Milbank, C.R., *New York Fashion*
(New York, 1989), p.22
2   Kelly, Rebecca J. 'Fashion in the Guilded Age',
Twentieth-Century American Fashion, p.16
3   Milbank, op. cit., p.46
4   Merkin, Daphne, 'Sometimes a Bag is Not Just
a Bag: Daphne Merkin on What Women Really
Want', Sunday Style Section, Spring 2006,
New York Times, 26 February 2006, p.234
5   Linda Fargo served as creative director for
visual presentation at Bergdorf Goodman for
over a decade. In 2006 Bergdorf Goodman
appointed Fargo to oversee the store's women's
fashion offerings as well.
6   'Mayor Bloomberg and Heidi Klum Announce
Measures to Support City's Garment and
Fashion Sector', Press Release 461-05,
12 December 2005, www.nyc.gov
7   The not-for-profit Garment Industry
Development Corporation (GIDC), which
describes itself as the link between designer
labels and high-quality producers, quotes
this statistic on their website, www.gidc.org
8   'New York City's Garment Industry: A New
Look?', New York Policy Institute, 2003, p.5
9   In September 2003 Mayor Michael Bloomberg
hosted a dinner at his home, at which the
CFDA/*Vogue* Fashion Fund was officially
announced. Between 2003 and 2004 the City's
own television channel produced and aired
18 episodes in a two-season series called
'Fashion in Focus', which aimed to feature
'the most pressing issues facing the industry'.
In December 2005 Bloomberg announced
a $244,000 grant for the training and
education of apparel workers.
10   This is generally accepted to be two to
five weeks for local manufacture compared
to eight to twelve for producing overseas.
11   EDFF winners mentioned in this book are
Zac Posen, As Four and Tess Giberson in
2002; Proenza Schouler and Cloak in 2003;
Derek Lam in 2004 and Mary Ping in 2005.
12   Gen Art also oversees an international design
competition open to emerging designers
(including students). It features its finalists in a
New York runway show. Winners receive $5,000.
13   Gehlhar, M. *The Fashion Designer Survival
Guide* (New York, 2005), p.156
14   Lost Art (2000), Zac Posen (2001) and
Duckie Brown (2003)
15   Past EDFF judges have included Sally Singer
(Fashion News/Features Director at *Vogue*),
Kim Hastreiter (Editor-in-Chief and Publisher
of *Paper*), Joan Kaner (Senior Vice President

and Fashion Director at Neiman Marcus),
Julie Gilhart (Vice President of Fashion
Merchandising at Barneys) and Ruth Finley
(Publisher of *The Fashion Calendar*). The
selections committee for menswear has
included Michael Bastian (Fashion Director
for Men's Store at Bergdorf Goodman), Jay
Bell (buyer for Menswear Designs at Barneys
New York) and Madeline Weeks (Fashion
Director at *GQ*). Past Gen Art judges have
included designers such as Cynthia Rowley,
Diane Von Furstenberg, Todd Oldham, Kate
Spade and Betsey Johnson, as well as many
of the same industry figures as the EDFF
including Joan Kaner and Julie Gilhart.
16   Designers are nominated by CFDA members,
fashion retailers, the press and stylists for
main garment categories such as womenswear,
menswear and accessories.
17   All references to *Vogue* are to American *Vogue*
unless specified otherwise.
18   According to the CFDA/*Vogue* Fashion Fund
press release of 15 October 2004 the criteria
for eligibility were to have a primary design
business in the United States in existence
for a minimum of two years; to have shown
evidence of talent through extensive editorial
coverage; to have demonstrated support from
key retailers; and to have a professional staff.
19   The 2004 selection committee consisted of
Peter Arnold, then Director of the CFDA;
Robert Duffy of Marc Jacobs; Julie Gilhart
of Barneys; the designer Narciso Rodriguez;
Stephen Ruzow of the apparel marketing firm
Kellwood; *Vogue*'s Fashion News/Features
Director Sally Singer, Senior Market Editor
Meredith Melling Burke and Editor-in-Chief
Anna Wintour.
20   *Vogue*, November 2004, Letter from the Editor.
21   The Fund finalists featured in this publications
are Derek Lam, Behnaz Sarafpour, Proenza
Schouler, Cloak, Jean Yu, Thom Browne and
Costello Tagliapietra.
22   Statistics for 2005–6 provided by *Vogue*'s
press office.
23   One of the magazine's editors, in describing
Vogue's aims for the Fund, suggested altruistic
motivation by stating '…it was not until I
became a judge for the CFDA/*Vogue* Fashion
Fund that I realized how vast and choppy is
the particular sea of troubles that this country's
premier fashion-design talents must navigate.
Personal debt, poverty, production delays,
myriad letdowns, customs snarls, even good,
old-fashioned weather… The Fashion Fund
is our riposte to the forces of destruction and
whimsy to which emerging designers are
particularly vulnerable.' *Vogue*, November
2004, p.441

24 These are the boundaries of the city's fashion district, according to the Fashion Center Business Improvement District, a not-for-profit organisation established in 1993 to promote New York City's apparel industry.
25 Interview with Susan Posen, 21 November 2005
26 Telephone interview with Ange of Three As Four, 2 December 2005
27 The area runs from Kenmore and Delancey streets on the north, East and Worth streets on the south, Allen street on the east, and Broadway on the west.
28 All quotes from Derek Lam in *New York Fashion in Context* taken from an interview with the author, 24 November 2005
29 The High Line ran from 35th Street down to St John's Park Terminal. Construction for the line began in 1929 and resulted in the ability to deliver goods straight to the receiving docks of factories and warehouses. From the late 1950s the structure suffered from years of disuse. Public campaigns were mounted to convert the High Line to public space. In late 2002, the City of New York began the process that would enable the High Line to be turned into a usable public space. The first section of the High Line is projected to open to the public in 2008. Press release, 'Friends of the High Line', 16 November 2005
30 New York City Landmarks Preservation Commission report, 'Gansevoort Market Historic District Designation Report, Part 1' on-line published version, http://www.nyc.gov/html/lpc/downloads/pdf/reports/gansevoortpt1.pdf, pp.19–20
31 New York City Landmarks Preservation Commission report, op. cit., p.163
32 All quotes from Alexandre Plokhov in *New York Fashion in Context* taken from an interview with the author, 30 November 2005
33 Interview with James Saunders, 18 May 2006
34 Email correspondence with the author, December 2005
35 Email exchange with Christian Joy, 2 August 2006

SPORTSWEAR CHIC

1 Author Mary Gehlhar wrote in her book, *The Fashion Designer Survival Guide* (Dearborn, 2005; pp.5–6), 'Although you are anxious to get out on your own, if you fail, you will end up working for someone else anyway. Do it now and increase your chance of success.' Gehlhar emphasizes the benefits of knowledge, connections and the building of reputation as well as capital that learning from an establishment designer provides.
2 Martin, R. *American Ingenuity, Sportswear 1930s–1970s* (London 1998), p.15
3 The designer supposedly insisted on pockets in every garment, for beyond their use for carrying things, pockets offered a lady 'a place to put one's hands so as not to feel ill at ease or vulnerable'. Yohanan, K. and N. Nolf, *Claire McCardell: Redefining Modernism* (New York 1998), p.51
4 Target Stores 2004 annual report indicated revenues of $46,839,000,000
5 Zac Posen quoted in 'Curvaceous' exhibition label text.
6 Louie, Elaine, 'For Zac Posen, a Refuge From the Runway', *New York Times*, 15 September 2005
7 According to Susan Posen, Zac's mother and business manager, foreign sales of Posen's clothing represents between 30% to 40% of their business.
8 All quotes from Zac Posen, unless indicated otherwise, come from an interview with the author in July 2005
9 Unless otherwise indicated all quotes from the designers come from a telephone conversation with Jack McCollough, 3 November 2005
10 *Vogue*, November 2004, p.427
11 Menkes, Suzy, 'The Collections/New York: As American's Mood Shifts, Downtown Style is Over.', *International Herald Tribune*, 11 September 2004
12 All quotes from Mary Ping come from an interview with the author, 11 October 2005
13 All quotes from Derek Lam come from an interview with the author, 29 November 2005
14 'The Shirtwaist' in Steele, V. (ed.), *Encyclopedia of Clothing and Fashion* (New York, 2005), pp.163–4
15 All quotes from the designer derive from a conversation with the author on 25 July 2005
16 Sarafpour confirmed the range as being between $1.5 and $2 million annually.

ATELIER

1 Conversation with the author on 3 November 2005
2 Bolton, A., *Wild: Fashion Untamed* (New York, 2005), p.13
3 Conversation with the author on 3 November 2005
4 All remaining quotes from Jordan Betten are taken from an interview with the author, 27 July 2005
5 Unless otherwise indicated all quotes from Jean Yu come from an interview with the author, 27 July 2005
6 Email exchange with Jean Yu, 5 December 2005
7 All quotes from Maggie Norris are taken from an interview with the author, 16 December 2005

8   All quotes are taken from conversations with the author on 28 November 2005 and 12 April 2006

9   Retailers carrying Costello and Tagliapietra from 2005 to 2006 included Barneys in New York, Le Bon Marché in Paris and Fred Segal in Los Angeles.

AVANT-GARDE

1   Bürger, P., *Theory of the Avant-Garde* (Chicago 1984), pp.84–89

2   Wilcox, C., *Radical Fashion* (London 2001), p.6

3   Slow and Steady Wins the Race website, www.slowandsteadywinstherace.com

4   Unless otherwise indicated all quotes from Slow and Steady's designer come from an interview with the author on 16 May 2005.

5   Telephone conversation with the author, 12 October 2005

6   Slow and Steady Wins the Race website, www.slowandsteadywinstherace.com

7   Unless otherwise indicated all quotes from Tess Giberson come from an interview with the author on 28 July 2005

8   Filmed interview with the designer on ivillage.com, 8 February 2004

9   All quotes from Three As Four come from an interview with the author on 27 July 2005

10 All quotes from Miguel Adrover come from a telephone interview on 6 December 2005

11 *New York Observer*, 28 February 2000

12 Evans, C., *Fashion at the Edge* (New Haven and London, 2003) p.253

13 Menkes, Suzy, *International Herald Tribune*, 8 February 2000

14 Bellafante, Ginia, 'The Year in Fashion, Before and After: Seeing Past the Cloud From Downtown', *New York Times*, December 25, 2001

15 Menkes, Suzy, 'Agony and Ecstasy on Runways of New York', *International Herald Tribune*, September 13, 2004

MENSWEAR

1   All quotes derive from a conversation with the author on 24 January 2006

2   Among VC Corporation's other holdings are Wrangler Jeans, Vanity Fair lingerie and the sportswear apparel company Nautica.

3   Although John Varvatos does design a small womenswear collection, it is sold only via the handful of John Varvatos stores.

4   Unless otherwise indicated all quotes from Daniel Silver and Steven Cox derive from an interview with the author on 25 July 2005

5   Email correspondence from the author, 9 January 2006

6   Unless otherwise indicated, all quotes from Alexandre Plokhov come from an interview with the author on 26 July 2005

7   Andy Comer interview with Plokhov, September 2005, on men.style.com, the online site for the men's magazines *GQ* and *Details*, http://men.style.com/fashion/style_notes/082605

8   Unless otherwise indicated all quotes from Thom Browne derive from an interview with the author on 27 July 2005

9   'Mister Thom Browne: New York City Tailor is Meatpacking District's Best Kept Secret', *Fantastic Man*, First Issue, Spring and Summer 2005, pp.15–26

10 'The Final Ten', *Vogue*, November 2005, p.368

11 These efforts include special skincare and cosmetic ranges, male-focused day spas, and beauty treatments.

CELEBRITY

1   Lubin, D.M., *Shooting Kennedy* (Berkeley, 2003)

2   Email correspondence with film and fashion historian Pamela Church Gibson, March 2006

3   Though Sprouse operated within the confines of New York's fashion industry (he presented catwalk shows during fashion week and had a store – briefly – in Soho), his punk-inspired, off-beat designs, along with his celebrity music connections, added an irreverent note to New York's fashion culture in the opulent 1980s.

4   Frere-Jones, Sasha, 'Positive Attitude: The Yeah Yeah Yeahs' new album', *The New Yorker*, 13 and 20 February 2006, p.172

5   All quotes from Karen Orzolek are from an interview with the author on 31 January 2006.

6   Interview with Emily Prichard, 16, London, 7 February 2006

7   All quotes from Christian Joy come from a telephone interview with the author, 18 January 2006

8   All quotes from Craig Robinson taken from a telephone interview 24 November 2005

9   *Blackbook*, Spring 2004, 'Bespoke Rocks the Garb'

10 In an interview with Jordan Betten (18 May 2005) the designer described Kravitz as a very loyal customer. Kravitz, according to Betten, has ordered so may Lost Art garments over the years – trousers, shawls, jewellery and other accessories – that he has dedicated a room in his house to display them.

11 'Indie Designers Pin Hopes (and Clothes) on Indie Singers', *New York Times*, 25 July 2004

12 All quotes from Ezra Reich are taken from telephone conversation with the author on 30 November 2005

13 Menkes, Suzy, 'The name game: can anyone
famous be a designer?', *International Herald
Tribune*, 14 September 2005

14 In 1993 Elle Macpherson launched her lingerie
line, 'Elle Macpherson Intimates'; in 2000
Chisty Turlington, with Puma, founded
'Nuala', her yoga-wear clothing line; Elizabeth
Hurley founded 'Beach', her swimsuit line,
in 2005.

15 Chandler, R and N. Chandler-Smith, 'Flava in
Ya Gear' in Welters, L. and P. Cunningham
(eds.), *Twentieth-Century American Fashion*,
(New York, 2005), p.232

16 Van Dyk Lewis, 'Hip-Hop Fashion' in Steele,
V. (ed.), *Encyclopedia of Clothing and Fashion*,
(New York, 2005), p.214

17 Simmons is the founder of Def Jam Records;
its early recordings included rap's first big acts,
such as Run D.M.C.. In a 2003 interview,
Simmons claimed that at the time the company
was founded, 1992, 'there was no such thing
as an urban clothing company. Now our
company is $300 million.' Mother Jones,
www.motherjones.com

18 diddyonline.com

19 Menkes, Suzy, 'The name game: can anyone
famous be a designer?', *International Herald
Tribune*, 14 September 2005

20 Figures provided by Paul Wilmot
Communications

21 This included Jennifer Lopez's 'Sweetface' line,
hip hop artist Jay-Z's Rock-A-Fella label and
singer Beyoncé Knowles' 'House of Dereon'.

22 All quoted from Gwen Stefani come from an
interview with the author on 20 January 2005

23 Menkes, Suzy, 'The name game: can anyone
famous be a designer?', *International Herald
Tribune*, 14 September 2005

24 Wilson, Eric, 'Her Name Already in
Lights, A Star Seeks Fashion Credibility',
11 February 2005

EPILOGUE
1 'Creative New York', a report published
on 18 December 2005 by Robin Keegan,
Neil Kleiman, Beth Siegel and Michael Kane;
http://www.nycfuture.org/images_pdfs/pdfs/
CREATIVE_NEW_YORK.pdf

SELECTED BIBLIOGRAPHY

Bürger, Peter, *Theory of the Avant-Garde* (Chicago, 1984)

Chambers, Bernice G., *Fashion Fundamentals* (New York, 1947)

Cullerton, Brenda, *Geoffrey Beene* (New York,1995)

Evans, Caroline, *Fashion at the Edge: spectacle, modernity and deathliness* (New Haven and London, 2003)

Gehlhar, Mary, *The Fashion Designer Survival Guide: an insider's look at starting and running your own fashion business* (New York, 2005)

Lee, Sarah Tomerlin (ed.), *American Fashion; The life and lines of Adrian, Mainbocher, McCardell, Norell, Trigere* (New York, 1975)

Lockwood, Charles, *Manhattan Moves Uptown: An illustrated history* (New York, 1976)

Lubin, David M., *Shooting Kennedy: JFK and the Culture of Images* (Berkeley and Los Angeles, 2003)

Martin, Richard, Sally Kirkland and Richard D. McComb, *All-American: A Sportswear Tradition* (New York, 1985)

Martin, Richard, *American Ingenuity: Sportswear 1930s-1970s* (London, 1998)

Martin, Richard, *Charles James* (New York, 1997)

Milbank, Caroline Rennolds, *New York Fashion: the evolution of American style* (New York, 1989)

Sischy, Ingrid, *Donna Karan: New York* (London, 1998)

Steele, Valerie (ed.), *Encyclopedia of Clothing and Fashion vols. i-iii* (Scribner Library of Daily Life) (New York, 2005)

Welters, Linda and Patricia A. Cunningham (eds.), *Twentieth-Century American Fashion* (New York, 2003)

Wilcox, Claire (ed.), *Radical Fashion* (London, 2001)

Yohannan, Kohle and Nancy Nolf, *Claire McCardell: Redefining Modernism* (New York, 1998)

Zinner, Nicholas, *I hope you are all happy now* (New York, 2005)

ACKNOWLEDGEMENTS

There are many people whose efforts and expertise have contributed to this book. First, I would like to thank all the designers mentioned. They all participated in lengthy interviews and then responded to many follow-up queries with genuine enthusiasm.

I am indebted to my colleagues in the V&A's Furniture, Textiles and Fashion Department: Linda Parry and Claire Wilcox for initially championing this project; and the continuing support of Christopher Wilk, Sarah Medlam, Leslie Miller, Susan North, Sue Prichard, Jenny Lister, Gareth Williams, Lucy Johnston, Charlotte Anderson, Suzanne Smith, Antonia Brodie, Victoria Carol, Catherine Flood, Sarah Grant, Kate Kaye, Helen Persson and Oliver Winchester. I would also like to thank colleagues in the Research Department, in particular Carolyn Sargentson, Christopher Breward, Julia Sachs and Victoria Coulson. I also thank student volunteer Samantha Safer for all her efforts. I also wish to acknowledge the unfailing efforts of Mary Butler and Frances Ambler in the V&A's Publications Department, Lisa Smith in Design, and Richard Davis and Peter Kelleher in the V&A's Photo Studio.

I am also grateful to Rebecca Arnold for her comments on this text and for sharing her considerable expertise. I thank Glenn Adams for his early suggestions on structure and methodology. I also thank my mother Silver Stanfill for her thorough readings of this text and my father Stanfill B. Stanfill for his thoughtful comments. I am grateful to Marcia Lee and family for welcoming me on my many trips to New York and to Katie Orenstein for introducing me to the talents of photographer Mara Catalan, to whom I am deeply grateful for her many images capturing the theatre of New York City's streets. I am also thankful for the patience and self-sufficiency of my husband and children.

I would like to express my appreciation to Paul Greenberg for sharing his expertise on contemporary music and to Mary Egan for her perspective on the dynamics of the retail industry. I also wish to thank the following experts for their shared insight into New York's young design talent: Andrew Bolton of the Costume Institute at the Metropolitan Museum of Art, Phyllis Magidson of the Museum of the City of New York, Valerie Steele of the Museum at F.I.T., Oriole Cullen of the Museum of London, Kelly Mills of Black and White Fashion, Miki Higasa of Kaleidoscope PR, Lisa Smilor of the CFDA, Mary Gehlhar of Gen Art, and Virginia Smith and Meredith Melling Burke of *Vogue*.

INDEX

Page numbers in italics refer
to illustrations

Adrover, Miguel 073, *073*,
086–9, *087*, 089
Armani, Giorgio 092, 102
As Four *see* Three As Four
Atelier=37 060

Baby Phat 120
Balenciaga 075
Barneys 011, 013, 030, 036,
042, 043, 046, 096, 098–9, 120
Beene, Geoffrey 010, *030*, 031, 067
Bergdorf Goodman 011, *011*,
042, 043, 064, 065, 103, 120
Betten, Jordan *see* Lost Art
Bloomingdale's 120
Browne, Thom 013, 092, 102–3,
102, 105
Burberry 036, 086

Carey-Williams, Robert 087
Cashin, Bonnie 010
Central St Martin's College of
Art and Design 034, 038, 088
Chanel 075
Cloak 012, 013, 015, 024–5,
092, 098–101, *101*
Club Monaco 102
Combs, Sean 'Diddy', for Sean
John 034, 108, 119–20, *119*
Costello, Jeffrey *see*
Costello Tagliapietra
Costello Tagliapietra 052, *066*,
067–9, *069*
Council of Fashion Designers
in America (CFDA) 012, 036,
087, 094
CFDA/*Vogue* Fashion Fund 012,
012, 033, 036, 042, 046, 060,
067, 098, 103
Perry Ellis Award 036, 087, 094, 120
Cox, Steven *see* Duckie Brown
Crow, Sheryl 057, *107*, 108, 116

de la Renta, Oscar 067
Dior, Christian 049
DKNY *082*
Doo-ri 012
Duckie Brown 024, *025*, *091*,
092, 096–7, *096*, 098

Ecco Domani Fashion
Foundation (EDFF) 012, *012*,
034, 041, 042, 067, 078

Fargo, Linda 011
Fashion Institute of Technology
(FIT) 11, 94
Funahashi, Jun *059*

Garza, Josh *114*
Gaultier, Jean Paul 108
Gen Art 012, 034, 056, 096
Giberson, Tess 073, 078–81,
079–80, 088
Gigli, Romeo 098
Gilhart, Julie 013, 098–9, 120
Greenfield, Martin 087
Gucci 075, 119

Hartnell, Norman 108
Hernandez, Lazaro *see*
Proenza Schouler
Hilfiger, Tommy 031, 064, 096, 119
Hobbs, Douglas 086

Imitation of Christ (IOC) 083
International Academy of
Merchandising and Design 098

Jacobs, Marc 012, 027, 082, 098
James, Charles 052, *052*
Jeffrey's 021, 103
Johnson, Betsy 108
Joy, Christian 027, *027*, 108,
110–113, *113*, 114, 119

Karan, Donna *030*, 031, 046
Kennedy, John F. 108
Klein, Anne 010, 033, 046
Klein, Calvin *030*, 031, 033,
094, 097
Kors, Michael 012, 042

L.A.M.B. 120, *120*
Lambert, Eleanor 11
Lam, Derek *012*, 013, 015,
021, 025, 030, 042–5, *042–5*,
046, 049
Lauren, Ralph *030*, 031, 064,
094, 096, 097, 119
London College of Fashion 038
Lopez, Jennifer 120
Lost Art 025, *025*, 052, 056–7,
056, 059, 060, 063, 064, 069,
107, 116

McCardell, Claire 010, 030, *030*, 049
McCollough, Jack *see* Proenza
Schouler
McLaren, Malcolm 108
Macy's 120
Margiela, Martin 075
Maxwell, Vera 010
Menkes, Suzy 036, 087, 088, 119
Milbank, Caroline Rennolds 010
Mizrahi, Isaac 012, 033, 046, *047*
Moschino 087

Norris, Maggie *011*, 052, 064–6,
064, 069

O (Orzolek), Karen 110–113, *113*

Parsons 011, *011*, 042
Pegasus (Leiber Group) 087, 088
Phat Farm 119, 120
Ping, Mary 012, *012*, 030,
038–41, *038–41*, 042, 049
Plokhov, Alexandre *see* Cloak
Posen, Zac 012, 013, 027, 030,
034–5, 034, 042, 046, 049
Potter, Clare 010
Proenza Schouler 0*12*, 030, 036–7,
036–7, 038, 042, 043, 046, 049

Reich, Ezra 116, *116*
Rhode Island School of
Design 078
Robinson, Craig 020, 108,
114–17, *114, 116*, 119
Rodriguez, Narciso 033, *033*
Rucci, Ralph 027, 052, *052*

Saks Fifth Avenue 120
Sarafpour, Behnaz 07, *012*, 029,
030, 046–9, *047–9*
Saunders, James 025
Shaver, Dorothy 011
Silver, Daniel *see* Duckie Brown
Simmons, Russell 119, 120
Slow and Steady Wins the Race
073, 074–5, *074, 076*, 078
Spade, Kate 082
Sprouse, Stephen 108
Stefani, Gwen 60, 120, *120*,
see also L.A.M.B.
Sui, Anna 056, 108

Tagliapietra, Robert *see*
Costello Tagliapietra
Teng, Yeohlee 052, *054*
Tennant, Stella *089*
Three As Four 018, *071*, 073,
082–5, *083–4*, 086
Toledo, Isobel 052, *054*
TSE 080

Varvatos, John 092, *093*, 094–5,
094–5, 096
Vassar College 038
Versace, Gianni 092
VF Corporation 094
Vogue 012–13, 036, 046, 060,
096, 098, 103

Westwood, Vivienne 108
Wintour, Anna 012

Yeah Yeah Yeahs 110–111
Yu, Jean 013, 027, *027*, *051*,
052, 060–63, 064, 069